TESTIMONIALS

· · · · · · · · · · · · · · · · · ·

The simple yet deep observations Jill shares in this book will get your people thinking, solving, and creating at a higher level.

—Gino Wickman
Author of *Traction* and
Entrepreneurial Leap

Too many entrepreneurial leaders and managers are getting bogged down with doing all the thinking in their companies, leading to burnout and low creativity. Using stories and practical applications—and her characteristic lightheartedness, energy, and optimism—Jill Young shows them how to teach their employees how to think, enabling them to move faster because everyone in the company will have their brain cells engaged in thinking at every level.

—Dan Sullivan
Cofounder of Strategic Coach®

The Thinking Advantage is a business book like no other. Jill is the expert on breaking complex leadership principles into practical and memorable steps. Her insights on creating a thinking organization are as astounding as they are applicable. Do yourself and your team a favor—read this book and get ready to collaborate, solve problems, and grow your company in a transformational way.

—Kary Oberbrunner
CEO of Igniting Souls and
Author of *Unhackable*

Every great Visionary and Integrator™ duo has a not-so-secret wish: for everyone in their company to do more thinking, problem solving, and idea generation. Too often, people mistakenly assume that their leaders are responsible for all of the thinking. In this book, Jill lays out four simple steps to get your whole company on board with learning, growing, and ultimately contributing to the long-term, greater good of the company.

—Mark C. Winters
Co-author of *Rocket Fuel*

This book had me from the first page! Our business leaders want and *need* thinkers on their teams. Here is how to get them. As with all other things, it isn't easy, but it's possible. Jill shows you how.

—Sara Stern
Certified EOS Implementer® and
Founder of The Sage Pages

You know you are leading when you experience others aligning their future with yours. This means that, at some level, they have thought through where you are going, agree with it, and are willing to go with you. To strengthen this alignment, we need to help folks think even better. *The Thinking Advantage* is a delicious, four-layer "How-to-Teach-Thinking Cake Box" filled with amazing icing and decoration recipes you can use to create your own cake.

—Walt Brown
Certified EOS Implementer® and
author of *The Patient Organization* and
Death of the Org Chart

Too many companies mindlessly continue to trudge forward with varying degrees of success. In this book, Jill provides a fantastic framework that allows leaders to thoughtfully raise emerging leaders around them with a framework for analysis that creates long-term success. Jill is spot-on with this encouraging book! Always one to quickly get to the essence of a situation, Jill delivers real-world solutions with practical application. *The Thinking Advantage* goes beyond informing and cements the learning objectives with structured reflection and a synopsis. Thanks, Jill, for once again making the complex simple for us! Onward!

—Rod Coleman
President of SYM Financial Advisors

Wow! *The Thinking Advantage* is incredible! It's chock full of practical insights and coaching wisdom. Jill adds fascinating context and historical data. She's hit it out of the park with this one!

—Shannon Waller
Entrepreneurial Team Strategist at Strategic Coach

In over 30 years of leading teams and managing companies, I've read the books, attended the workshops, and mostly what I've learned is that I still have a lot to learn. The hard part these days is knowing which of those learning opportunities to say *yes* to. In my six-year coaching career, I can without hesitation say that whenever Jill Young has something to share, it's time to start listening. If you're an entrepreneur who wants to grow and get better, reading *The Thinking Advantage* needs to go to the top of your list.

—John McMahon
Certified EOS Implementer® and
Founder of The Traction Group

Not only will *The Thinking Advantage* teach you how to turn your people into thinkers, it will help you see what a gift work truly is. This book reminded me of what makes me happy and fulfilled professionally; I love coaching, and Jill captures the essence of it in this book. I can now envision what it would be like to run an organization of thinkers; I can't wait to start implementing her ideas.

—Jim Burns
President of Corporate Floors

I love the way Jill breaks down the steps, algorithms, and modes in this book. They are presented in a way that's easy to understand. I have more than a few takeaways to incorporate into my training and onboarding Rocks. What I've learned goes beyond business and I know will help me personally as well.

—Martha Diaz
Head of Finance at Smile Fort Worth

Wow! Wow! Wow! Jill's book definitely speaks to me. There are hundreds of nuggets throughout this book. The stories Jill tells are real and she adds a fun dimension in addition to "Lived it"—"Done it"—"Not Theory"—this stuff is real.

—Bobi Siembieda
Certified EOS Implementer®

I loved the book and could not put it down. Jill has produced an incredibly insightful book that can help teams work better together, enhancing the success of the company!

—Ronald Johnsey
Founder and CEO of ThinkWhy

Jill has done it again! She has thoughtfully created another method of challenging us to think and be better! Imagine if each of us took quality time to think! Imagine what our lives and world would become. The strategies created and shared in this book are perfect for our lizard brains to comprehend and use.

—Sonya Jury
Professional EOS Implementer®

Encouraging people to think, to problem solve, to bring their best is so rewarding (when it works). Jill has taken a trove of sprawling, rich information and made it both simple and actionable. If you've been growing your leadership skills for a long time, you are bound to get reinvigorated by this review of the essentials—and a few great new tools. If you're newer to the fascinating practice of getting people to do what you want them to do, here's your handbook. Start applying it now!

—Lynda Martin
Professional EOS Implementer®

Jill got me again! She leads with a story that grabbed my attention, and by the third paragraph, I knew exactly what to expect to learn from this book!

—Christian Landers
Chief Operating Officer and
Integrator of LSR Multifamily

In *The Thinking Advantage*, Jill Young builds upon the Coaching Magic foundation of her first two books. In our work as EOS Implementers, we help managers become better leaders; implicit in this is the fact that great leaders must also be great coaches for their teams. *The Thinking Advantage* outlines a simple coaching algorithm. I highly recommend this valuable handbook and reference for all leaders who seek to sharpen their coaching skills.

—Alex Freytag
Certified EOS Implementer, Speaker,
Author of *Achieve Your Vision*, and
co-author of *Profit Works*

If you have an interest in improving the thinking skills in your organization, this book is for you. A valuable thought leadership piece about ... thinking, and Jill's writing is fun and approachable. Are you stuck in a never-ending tactical loop? Jill's thinking algorithms offer incredible value. Read them. Master them. Put them to work. Your entire organization will be thinking differently in no time.

—Victoria Cabot
Certified EOS Implementer® and
Founder of Velocity 6 Leadership

Other Books by Jill Young

*The Earning Advantage: 8 Tools You Need
to Get Paid the Money You Want*

*The Courage Advantage: 3 Mindsets Your Team
Needs to Cultivate Fierce Discipline, Incredible
Fun, and a Culture of Experimentation*

The
Thinking
Advantage

4 Essential Steps Your Team
Needs to Cultivate
Collaboration, Leverage
Creative Problem-Solving, and
Enjoy Exponential Growth

JILL YOUNG

The Thinking Advantage: 4 Essential Steps Your Team Needs to Cultivate Collaboration, Leverage Creative Problem-Solving, and Enjoy Exponential Growth © 2020 by Jill Young. All rights reserved.

Published by Author Academy Elite
PO Box 43, Powell, OH 43065
www.AuthorAcademyElite.com

Library of Congress Control Number: 2020911988

Softcover: 978-1-64746-349-6
Hardcover: 978-1-64746-350-2
E-book: 978-1-64746-351-9

Also available on audiobook.

To my sons.
Your creative and abundant thinking
brings me the greatest joy.

CONTENTS

Introduction
xvii

The Case for Thinking in Your Company
xix

The Four Steps
xxiii

STEP ONE: TEACH
1

Teaching Adults
6

Eight Approaches for Adult Learners
13

Practical Applications
22

What We've Learned
30

STEP TWO: COACH
33

What is Coaching?
35

The Coaching Magic Matrix
39

Observe Mode
49

Respond Mode
58

Co-Create Mode
86

Return and Reflect Mode
106

STEP THREE: DON'T RESCUE
109

A More Thoughtful Hero
111

Don't Take the Monkey!
112

When You Can See Farther Down The River
119

The Fire Department Tool
123

STEP FOUR: RETURN AND REFLECT
129

Experience is a Hot Commodity!
131

Return: Make the Invitation!
133

Reflect: Hold Regular Reflection Sessions
135

Reflect: Types of Reflection Sessions
138

Reflect: Teach Someone Else
141

Conclusion
149

Acknowledgments
153

Appendices
155

INTRODUCTION

My heart dropped. A company I was coaching had just rolled out their ambitious new vision for the future with the tools and a plan to get there, and I was excited to hear how it went. When the owner called me, he reported that one manager approached him after the rollout and exclaimed, "It seems like you want me to do way more than I used to do. I don't get paid enough to think; I just want to do what I'm told."

I don't get paid enough to think ... I don't get paid enough to think ... I don't get paid enough to think ... The phrase repeated over and over again in my head. I couldn't sleep! I couldn't understand how a human couldn't *want* to think, be dissatisfied with being *asked* to think, or be *repulsed* by the notion of being creative and solving problems. Unable to wrap my thinking around it caused me physical pain!

This is when I had my "aha" moment. Maybe we haven't taught people *how* to think. If I replaced the word *think* with a different skill, like painting, would I be so offended? If that manager had said, "I don't get paid enough to paint," where would my brain go then? Well, I guess I'd say, "Let's teach him to paint!"

That was the origin of this book. If our new world of work needs more thinkers and solvers, let's teach our people *how* to think by becoming a thinking organization!

The effects of the global events of 2020 have only added fuel to our innovation, and in the wake of looming and unprecedented problems, we have been called to bigger and better thinking.

There was something of a "great awakening" as society, en masse, had to think differently and find *immediate* solutions for problems that emerged overnight. Working from home, family schedules, childcare, education, and communicating with friends and family—all of these things changed in an instant. For the first time in a long time, we all had to *rethink* everyday life, and the creativity we witnessed was inspiring. From reviving the one-room (at-home) schoolhouse approach to education, to restaurants pivoting to contactless takeout and delivery, to the retooling of manufacturing plants virtually overnight, everything changed so quickly.

The upside of these interesting times was that most people had a chance to engage in thinking again. If we can apply the learning from this collective experience to our future, we'll find more possibilities for upward mobility for individuals and companies. This potential is truly unlimited if we can evolve our workforce to engage in more thinking. Now is the time to take the thinking skills once saved for the elite (philosophers, emperors, nobles, bosses, and knowledge workers) and unlock them for everyone in our organization to create a better future together. Some say that information is now a commodity, as it's widely available to most people. I believe that it's how we think about and use that information that will pull us forward into the Era of Thinking.

Throughout this book, we'll discover why now, with fierce urgency, the Era of Thinking has arrived, how to create a company full of thinkers who can collaborate and continually improve themselves and those around them, and how you as their leader can usher in thinking as a part of your company's culture. As Napoleon Hill said, "You can think your way into or out of almost any circumstance, good or bad."

THE CASE FOR THINKING IN YOUR COMPANY

It appears that since 1850 or so, critical thinking has steadily worked its way up the list of our most valuable assets. It has become our best tool! *Think and Grow Rich* by Napoleon Hill, published in 1937, was the first mainstream book that introduced the concept of "thought as power" to the elite. The book has sold over 200 million copies, communicating Hill's novel ideas to the masses. In the book, Hill states, "Start with thinking."

One of my favorite phrases is "the fastest thinker wins." If this is true (and I believe it is), as leaders we have everything to gain from teaching our people *how to think*. Traditionally, we assigned the burden of thinking to leadership only; we expected only leaders to do the hard thinking. Just as we delegate the *doing* throughout the organization as we learn to navigate new technologies and complexities, *thinking* can no longer be a skill reserved only for top leadership. It needs to be a skill taught throughout the entire organization. When we've taught our people how to think and they've mastered the skill, then—as with any skill—they'll get better and faster at thinking.

Unfortunately, most of the people in our organizations lack the skill of critical thinking. It could be that children and young adults aren't learning how to think in schools, churches, and homes, and there are certainly opportunities to change curricula and priorities in these civic structures. But in the meantime, capitalists need more thinkers in their organizations, and I believe entrepreneurial companies are ripe catalysts to teach thinking. Why? We're scrappy and can try things quickly without worrying about perfection, and we hit the ground running. We also have the most to gain. If we can create thinkers out of all of the people in our entrepreneurial companies, the people will have an exponential effect on each other. Their efforts will multiply!

At the time of writing, I've spent the last six years coaching leadership teams in the US and Canada through more than 600 sessions. During these sessions, I have witnessed that when teams learn how to *think*, they solve issues and make decisions faster, thereby creating a powerful team that generates additional thinkers. As an Expert EOS Implementer®, I have the unique privilege of guiding leaders and companies using the Entrepreneurial Operating System® (EOS®). EOS is a set of proven and timeless tools that helps leadership teams think about and make decisions about the vision of the company, create an accountable and disciplined company that has Traction®, and encourage an open, honest, and healthy culture. When these companies embrace the EOS tools and the coaching, they elevate their thinking and the speed of their success. This book will reveal the mystery of this thinking process.

I've organized this book for use as an algorithm. An algorithm is a set of steps that, when followed, will get you the same result every time. When my son Tyler was nine, he brought home a Rubik's Cube and said, "Watch what I can do." In 56 seconds, he solved the puzzle. I thought I had a genius on my hands, but I later realized that Tyler had discovered the power of YouTube. He watched videos that taught him the secret to solving the Rubik's Cube. The "secret" (an algorithm) was a set of steps that he repeated until the puzzle was solved.

The concept of algorithms originated in math and science and is now relied upon heavily in technology and computer sciences. So algorithms are not new, but humanity is starting to use them in new ways, applying them in our companies (in the form of processes) and in our lives (in the form of habits).

We use many algorithms every day without even realizing it. The formula for getting a mathematical average is an algorithm, and so is every recipe you've ever followed. Each recipe is a finite list of instructions used to create something or perform a task. James Clear, in his book *Atomic Habits*, gives his readers formulas or algorithms to form and break habits. Yuval Noah Harari even stated in *21 Lessons for the 21st Century* that an algorithm's concept is the most important concept we have as homo sapiens!

When we apply this concept of an algorithm to human behavior, I suggest that we define it as "a series of steps that, when followed, will result in your desired outcome *over time*." Because humans are dynamic, changing, and not always rational creatures, we need repetition and muscle memory for our algorithms to stick. The Thinking Advantage is simply a four-step algorithm that, when applied over time, will result in a company full of thinkers. This company can stay ahead of issues, solve those issues, overcome its obstacles, and serve customers in an ever more creative and valuable way. You'll also find that I've embedded some algorithms within the algorithm to help you master each step!

TEACH

COACH

DON'T RESCUE

RETURN & REFLECT

THE FOUR STEPS

Here is a high-level overview of the four essential steps of the Thinking Advantage algorithm:

Step One: Teach – In this step, you'll provide your workforce with the instructional and informational building blocks of their jobs and set them up with all the tools they will need to be productive. I'll show you how to teach in a way that really sticks because we know that without engaging training, the rest of the algorithm is difficult and time-consuming. Teaching effectively is the first step—it's the foundation.

Step Two: Coach – In this step, you'll build on the teaching by engaging your team's brains in problem solving and ideation. They will have the opportunity to implement what they have learned from the first step in real life. If the training is the science, the coaching is the art. It's the fine-tuning of the basics, the encouragement of deeper understanding on an individual level that will transform the way your people think and interact with each other.

Step Three: Don't Rescue – In this step, you will learn to understand and master your own behaviors and thinking patterns so that your people have more opportunity for rich growth experiences with success *and* failure. When your people have responsibility for their own actions, they'll increase their capabilities and their confidence. This will enhance the way they think about future obstacles and opportunities.

Step Four: Return and Reflect – In this simple yet powerful step, you'll create a space where your people can reflect on their experiences so the learning will stick. We'll use what we know about the biology of the brain to help them identify and simplify their learning so they can generalize those lessons for the next experience they'll undoubtedly have. By using this step, we start to make thinking an addictive habit!

Before jumping into these four steps, fill out the scorecard below, or complete the digital version at JillYoung.com. Do it once now, and come back to it often to self-assess how you are applying the Thinking Advantage.

The Thinking Advantage SCORECARD
for use with *The Thinking Advantage* by Jill Young

STATEMENTS	1	2	3	4	5	6	7	8	9	10	11	12	Score	Goal
Teach	Your people only need the basics in order to do their job. Once they learn them, they really don't need any additional teaching.			You'd love to spend more time teaching your people, but never seem to prioritize it.			You spend time and money on formal training, which has been in place for years. Multiple outside experts ensure the training is high quality.			Your teaching goes beyond skills and productivity improvements—it's about collaborative thinking. You update and adapt, and people learn daily.				
Coach	You expect that if you hire people to do a job, they will do it. You don't have time to make sure they are doing it right. It's up to them.			You get frustrated when you need to spend time supporting your people. You often get behind on your projects because others need direction.			You're the single source of information for your people. They rely on you for advice and regularly comment that your direction is vital.			You often have brief conversations with your people and ask questions to help them think through their problems. You want them to be their best.				
Don't Rescue	It's easier to do the job yourself than it is to worry about someone else doing it wrong.			You know that letting people fail helps them grow, but there's a big risk of things being done wrong. You take on most of the hard things.			The hard things are your job. It's why you get paid more—others don't have the knowledge. You delegate some things, but not critical tasks.			Your employees learn from their experiences and are able to accept additional accountability. It's hard not to take over, but you encourage instead.				
Return and Reflect	You are so busy that taking time to rehash the past just isn't a priority. You move on and try to forget the past.			You change processes and update training after a miss, but you aren't getting to the root of issues. It's frustrating—the misses are repeated.			You have a formal annual review. You file results but rarely have deep conversations about them. You rely on lots of reporting.			You regularly ask the question, "What did we learn?" often followed by rich conversations that produce permanent and foundational change.				

STEP ONE
TEACH

TEACH

COACH

DON'T
RESCUE

RETURN&
REFLECT

Imagine that you and a friend are having a picnic by the side of a river. Suddenly, you hear a shout from the direction of the water—a child is drowning! Without thinking, you both dive in, grab the child, and swim to shore. Before you can recover, you hear another child crying for help. You and your friend jump back in to rescue her as well. Then, another struggling child drifts into sight ... and another ... and another. The two of you can barely keep up! Suddenly, you see your friend wading out of the water, about to leave you alone. "Where are you going?" you cry.

Your friend answers, "I'm going upstream to tackle the guy who's throwing all these kids in the water."

This story is adapted from a public health parable commonly attributed to Irving Zola, an American writer and medical sociologist. I told a version of the story for years, usually at the beginning of my Accountability Activator workshops. One day, while reading *Upstream* by Dan Heath, I was thrilled to discover the story (as retold here with its original attribution). Dan is one of my favorite thinkers and authors, and in his book, he calls this proactive or preventive approach to problem-solving "going upstream."

In business, we are successful to the degree that we can prevent, predict, and solve issues. Heath's research shows that companies often choose to resolve issues as they arise instead of taking the upstream approach. It's easier to measure the output of solved matters than it is to measure what never happened because you prevented it. Since business owners currently seem to be obsessed with data, we believe that it's hard to prove if something isn't easily measured. If it's hard to prove, it gets less attention and investment. In this first step of our Thinking Advantage algorithm, Teach, we'll swim upstream to see who is pushing all these people in the water without first teaching them to swim.

I'll argue that investing in teaching our people must be the first step. As with solving the Rubik's Cube, you can't expect the subsequent steps to go as planned without accurately taking the correct first step. This is what a lot of growing companies experience. Because the teaching was done poorly in the past, there are a lot of issues to clean up, causing their leaders to say, "We don't have time to train our people." But if we first invest in training our people, there will be less mess to clean up later. By teaching our people, we give them space to pre-think, pre-plan, and pre-observe obstacles they may encounter and find strengths they can rely on.

As Patrick Lencioni states in his book *The Five Dysfunctions of a Team*, "Because teams are made up of imperfect human beings, teams are inherently dysfunctional." (Human beings? Raise your hand if that's you. Oh good—me too!) To combat the natural dysfunction of human beings, companies have been known to create extensive training programs. Training is nothing new to business. In fact, *Training Magazine* reports that in 2019, businesses (both large and small) spent $83 billion on training.

When I started managing the family business at age 19, one of the first projects I kicked off was an internal training program. I didn't do it because I knew how important training was but because I loved learning and assumed everyone else did too. I was also in the middle of a BS degree in psychology and was motivated by a professor's fascinating research on how we learn.

So, armed with a bit of authority, I set out to create a comprehensive training plan. My first approach was to write—from scratch—a library of what to do and how to do it manuals. Halfway through my fourth topic, I got bored and needed a shortcut, so I asked others in my professional association to share their training with me. They did, but it didn't feel like our way of doing things. So, on a very high-tech Commodore 64, I rewrote the manuals. After months of this torture, it was time to deliver the training handbook. I stood in front of my employees and read the documents to them, knowing things would be different the next day. We'd be a better, more efficient company!

As I retell that story, hindsight makes me laugh at my 19-year-old self who expected the angels to sing after all the hard work I'd done! The training session was a flop. No one asked any questions afterward, so I thought everyone got it—they didn't. I learned more about what *not* to do during that experience with training than what *to* do.

Decades later, as president of a growing and expanding CPA firm, I jumped into the training arena again. This time, I applied more of what actually works (without knowing it). When I held this role, I viewed my lack of accounting and finance knowledge negatively. In reflection, I think it was an asset and helped me develop skills and build my own capabilities.

I was acutely aware that I couldn't create a training program on my own. The information had to come from the people already working in the company. I started a series of interviews with our talented staff and took a checklist approach to document the training. As the staff listed what was necessary to learn and know, I wrote it down. After organizing the topics, I found a champion for each subject and asked them to write some simple descriptions and instructions. By doing this, we completed the training manual. The subject champions then taught their sections to the rest of the staff, and we all agreed it worked!

My next aha moment came after I hired three people to start on the same day, all in different positions. I knew I couldn't spend the day with all three of them at the same time, so I improvised and told them they were all in charge of their own training. They saw who the champions were for each topic, and it was the new employees' job to make appointments with those champions to complete their training. I suggested they check things off as they went and report back to me a week later to let me know how they had fared.

I found out by accident that adults learn best when they are in charge of their learning and when they have input on what goes into the training, both of which I facilitated unintentionally.

TEACHING ADULTS

Not all thinkers learn the same way, and it's beneficial to acknowledge that adults learn differently than children. When most of us think of teaching and learning, we have a picture in our mind of a classroom. We picture a teacher at the front and students at their desks looking to the teacher for wisdom. Some adult trainings still use this childhood approach to teaching.

One of my proudest accomplishments is completing two degrees while working full-time. I've always been an active person, so I don't even remember making the decision to go to school full-time and work full-time; it just happened.

Upon reflection, I realize that the two degrees were very different. I earned my bachelor's degree in psychology at a traditional university, where my learning environment felt very similar to my high school. I listened as the teacher taught our lesson. Then I did my homework, took the tests, and got a B+. (I double-dog dare you to ask me about my B+ theory!) When I graduated with that degree, I was so mentally and physically exhausted, I declared, "I will never go back to school!" With an eight-month-old baby and a full-time job, I'm sure you can see that was a pretty solid declaration.

A year later, when I signed up for an MBA at the University of Phoenix on a bit of a whim and on a high of my own ambition, my friends and family justifiably questioned my sanity. However, I trudged along obediently, taking one course after another, and I fell in love with my courses at the University of Phoenix. The very first class of my very first course was an interactive-type that required my opinion (which I was asked for), and my thoughts through a case study. I was asked to answer thought-provoking questions and apply the first lessons to my business in the next week. Classes were held on Mondays from 6:00 p.m. to 10:00 p.m., and I recall rarely sleeping on Monday nights because my brain wouldn't turn off!

The difference between these two experiences is that the University of Phoenix was designed with adults in mind. Wouldn't it be cool if all your training inspired people in your company so much that they couldn't stop thinking?

Eight Elements of Adult Learning

Let's examine these eight elements of adult learning to see what we can apply to our training programs.

1. Adults learn best with a little bit of structure and a lot of autonomy.

When the teacher has all the control over the learning environment (seating, agenda, test dates, class times, the length of the topic), and the student has very little, there tends to be a lot of memorization and repetition required for information to sink in. This is how most of us were taught in school, and we probably recall lots of memorization and repetition! This type of learning will help us remember facts, formulas, and vocabulary words, but there is rarely a deeper purpose.

Adults learn the opposite way. They learn best when they have some control over the learning environment. For example, adults like to know the training's objectives but learn better with a flexible agenda so they can spend more time on certain topics when needed. They learn best when they can direct the learning and actively create the agenda, going as quickly or as slowly as they need to. One way to provide this autonomy is to have a menu of topics in the curriculum rather than listing them in a set order. Remove obstacles that would require adult learners to master one concept before moving to another when it doesn't make sense.

2. Adults learn best when they have a specific need to fulfill or real-world problems to solve.

Adults are busy, and their brains are already full. To retain information, it needs to make it through an efficiency filter in the mind that asks, *Is this relevant enough to give it my attention?* If there isn't a need, it's tough to engage an adult learner and, therefore, hard to make the training stick. Consider how interested you are when your boss says, "This Wednesday is required sales tax compliance training." If you're like most people, you think, *Ugh, I have so much to do! This is a waste of my time!* That's where the learning is sabotaged. However, if you've just lost your potential to earn your annual bonus because of several mistakes you made when charging sales tax, this is the type of training you'll most likely engage with, and you'll retain the knowledge. Adults are motivated to gain the knowledge that will help them fix their current issues.

3. Adults learn best when they can apply the learning right away.

If the training is too far removed from its practical application, the effectiveness of the training is poor. Consider the sales tax training from the previous example. If the training is this Wednesday but you won't use the knowledge until the end of the quarter, there's a big chance that the information will be lost by the time you're ready to apply it. Teams who understand this create training opportunities or refresher courses close to the event. As a bonus, a training close to the day of the event/test also increases adults' confidence in positive performance. If adults need to wait even a week, their confidence in their performance is lower. Leaders who invest in training get the activity started right away.

4. Adults learn best by doing.

The best adult learning environments get the learners' hands on the tools or concepts as soon as possible. Instead of the teacher talking for an hour before the learner does anything, the teacher gives a quick micro lesson and gets the group working right away. Active learning, trial and error, and little successes are also important for keeping adults engaged. I recently started taking painting classes. In the first five minutes of my first lesson, I placed my paint-covered brush on the canvas. My instructor knew the faster she had me paint, the more I'd engage with the concepts and better understand them. Role-playing, putting your hands on the tools, and working the formulas are examples of learning by doing.

5. Adults learn best when there is plenty of opportunity for reflection and conversation.

Yes, adults learn better when we can get our hands on the project quickly, but we also need to reflect on what we're experiencing and processing in our minds. This can come from talking about it, writing about it, and thinking about it. Great instructors create a space for this reflection time. "Does anyone have any questions?" is usually a throw-away sentence—as in *trash!*—that teachers or presenters *hope* no one answers. Q&A time built into learning programs and workshops is there to create space for reflection. Interspersing this Q&A throughout the lesson and upgrading it by asking reflection-based questions during the lesson is more effective than leaving conversation until the end. Reflection-based questions posed by effective leaders are discussed thoroughly in Step Four: Return and Reflect.

6. Adults learn best when they can see what needs to be done.

If the teacher explains concepts rather than showing the learners how to complete the task, disengagement and confusion often occur. When you're teaching a concept, things like stories, analogies, and models can help adult learners see what's required. Don't just tell, *show*.

7. Adults learn best through collaboration with others.

This is because of the Mastermind Effect. I was first introduced to the Mastermind Effect when I read the book *Think and Grow Rich* by Napoleon Hill. (OMG, I almost wrote *Napoleon Dynamite*! Feel free to laugh! Adults like laughter while learning too.) Hill claims that one of the habits of successful business leaders is that they surround themselves with people with whom they can talk through their issues. Having conversations and considering other viewpoints helps us get to solutions faster. When designing your training programs, consider adding more group exercises and discussions. Adults love to learn from each other. As we mature, adults move from an *I-must-do-it-myself* mentality to loving the insight, solutions, and aha moments that collaboration brings.

Every so often, I have a leader in a training session who still wants to do most things in isolation, earn his grade, or be the best in the class. These individuals are usually on the brink of a maturing moment and, if shown the benefits of collaboration, often embrace it. I rarely see individuals who refuse to collaborate after experiencing its benefits. When I find them, they don't stay employed in fast-growing, successful companies for very long. As a byproduct of collaboration-based learning, I've noticed that teams who learn together often get more out of the training.

For several years, I've offered my Accountability Activator workshop in two different formats. One format is for a single company that brings 5 to 50 leaders, managers, and rising stars to the workshop. The other format is designed for leaders and managers of multiple companies to be in the same workshop. I've observed that the skills and depth of application are better retained in the multiple-company format where the *leaders train together*. I think this is because they start with a deeper trust of each other; they can hold each other accountable for the commitments they make during training and learning. When we all know the concepts and can discuss them later, the training is more likely to stick. These leaders know that they brought their best, and their colleagues brought their best too.

8. Adults learn best when they teach.

Yes! In the act of teaching someone how to do something, the teacher learns too. Practitioners in the medical field use the phrase "watch one, do one, teach one" when training medical students. They know that teaching a concept to another person is a great way to facilitate additional or deeper learning. I see companies doing this by asking *newer* people in the company to take part in the orientation of the company's *newest* people. This requires them to teach the company history, culture, or processes close to when they first learned them.

In entrepreneurial companies, we're tempted to think, *We don't have time to train.* In the rest of this chapter, I'll give you some ideas for how you can effectively and thoroughly teach your people in the least amount of time possible. We're also tempted to make the excuse, *What if I train my people and they leave?* This makes way for us to argue with ourselves because we respond to our excuse with, *What if I don't train my people and they stay?* Let's take a minute to answer that rhetorical, decade-old question.

REFLECTION SECTION

1. What if I train my people and they leave? What's the worst that could happen? How would we suffer if trained people left?

_____

_____

_____

_____

2. What if I don't train my people and they stay? What's the worst that could happen? Who will suffer if untrained people stay on?

_____

_____

_____

_____

Here's a reminder about humans: we're efficient beings. We'll find the easiest route from point A to point B. Point B is most often where we have our needs met. Often, this means that when we're left to do something without instruction, we'll do it the way that comes most naturally (easiest) to us. If you're trying to run a smooth company, everyone doing it their way won't work for long, especially as you grow.

You need to be aligned with how you're building your product, delivering it to your customers, communicating with each other, and solving your issues. These aren't the easiest things to do, especially when you take several humans with different natural abilities and ask them to agree on one way. Just thinking about that blows my mind! How do we get anything done at all? But we can and do, and when we create thinkers in our company, we generate amazing results. These results start with a dedication to teaching our people how to think.

EIGHT APPROACHES FOR ADULT LEARNERS

Here are eight approaches to make your training more effective for adult learners in an entrepreneurial world:

1. Assign Pre-Work

Before the actual teaching event, ask people to do some pre-work. Pre-work can come in the form of questions to think about, data to gather and bring, expressed expectations of the course, samples to share, or—my favorite—a sloppy paragraph filled with what they already know about the topic. During the pre-work phase, the prepared content can give the instructor insight into what's important to the group. The instructor can then adjust the agenda or make recommendations. But the big effect here is that the pre-work prepares adult learners' minds for the topic. It's warming up the brain for training like we warm up our bodies before a big workout. A good pre-work exercise gets the brain ready to learn.

2. Start with Mindset

Mindset is simply how we think about a subject. The purpose is to get the learner engaged with the topic at a higher level or see the problem from a bigger, longer-term perspective so they'll understand why you're investing in this training. When practical, this mindset assessment step also connects the learner emotionally and individually to the material or topic.

For example, I used a story at the beginning of this book about two friends who kept rescuing children out of the river. I wanted to help you see how swimming upstream to teach your people how to think was a worthy goal. And it worked because you're still reading this book! ☺ Learners need to see the topic in a high-level, critical-thinking way to really understand it. It's all about the *why*. Why are we here today? Here are a few methods that I often rely on:

Stories

Stories are reliable ways to engage learners and help them reset their mindsets. Stories with personal or emotional elements have extra power. There are dozens of stories in this book specifically shared to invite you to think about the topic from a deeper perspective or to get you out of a thinking pattern that may be harmful.

Mental Models

Mental models have a way of simplifying our thinking. Many of these mental models prompt the question in the learner's mind, *Where am I in this model?* Although we're careful not to attach labels to people, mental models do have validity in getting us to think about our behavior or thinking. The Coaching Magic Matrix is an example of a mental model. It's found on Page 39 of this book. It'll help you define where you are and where you want to be as a coach. (More mental models can be found on my website at JillYoung.com.) Coaches love mental models, and I'm no exception! A 2x2 mental model (like the one I present in this book) is one of my favorite tools to create and share with my clients.

Fun

Sometimes, engaging someone in thinking about a concept in a new way can be done with lightheartedness and fun. When it is tied to a point, playing a game, telling a joke, or having a contest can engage the brain differently.

A classic game that reinforces the importance of communication is the telephone game. This is where the instructor whispers a statement to the first person in the line, then they whisper that same statement to the next person in the line, and that continues until you get to the end of the line. The last person tells the group what they heard, and we often laugh because the statement has become so twisted. This kind of game helps the learner pause to think about communication at a higher level.

3. Teach an Algorithm

The third approach to make your training more effective is to teach an algorithm. An algorithm is simply the steps to follow to get your desired outcome. Algorithms (used in the field of mathematics) take something very complex and simplify it for the user. Just as Tyler discovered the algorithm for solving a Rubik's Cube, you can offer your people a simple three-to-seven-step process for a topic. Think of this step as offering them the high-level, bullet-pointed steps to follow so they don't need to figure it out on their own.

Unless the algorithm you're teaching is mathematics- or science-based, it only needs to work 80% of the time. This means you won't need to invest in teaching all of the exceptions. They'll discover them on their own during the practice phase, and you can help them through the exceptions when you're coaching.

An example of this is using your documented core processes as your algorithm. If you've followed the 3-Step Process Documenter™ as part of the EOS Toolbox™, you already have this algorithm defined for training on processes. Demonstrating the algorithm as you're sharing it helps the learner see it in action. Using examples, videos, or showing them how the steps fit together helps the next step—practicing—become more valuable.

4. Facilitate Practice

As quickly as possible, get the learners practicing with the algorithm you just shared. If you're training on a machine, make sure the machine is available. If you are teaching a concept, have case studies on hand to discuss. If you're training a physical skill, make sure they get their hands on the tools early in the process. Effective practice involves role-play, putting pieces together, practicing with the tools, finding obstacles, repeating, and doing it the wrong way. This helps us implement the idea introduced in the training to a process that affects our daily productivity.

5. Discuss Challenges

After the learner has practiced with the concepts, tools, or new skill, save some space for discussing the challenges they faced, real or imagined. This is where the big thinking starts. They've been taught the algorithm, seen how it works, and practiced with it—they're bound to have some thoughts on how it went.

When you ask them to discuss these thoughts, they learn in a deeper way. The learning becomes sticky! Hearing from the other people in the class also brings up new thoughts and challenges to ponder. Often, the instructor can offer additional examples, stories of exceptions, and ask powerful questions to the group to clear up misunderstandings.

It's been my experience that this is the step where the aha moments occur. I've found that discussions in small groups (three to seven people) can also engage each learner in a way that's unique to them and allow everyone the chance to speak. Larger group discussions (eight or more) only allow for a few to share their thoughts. The power in this type of conversation comes by asking participants to actively look for failure points. This will help them see future obstacles and fill the gaps in their understanding.

6. Encourage Commitment

This step is all about commitment to action. Most likely, the learner will leave the training expected to apply what they learned with very little oversight. By asking them to make a commitment, write it down, and share it with the class, the action is more likely to happen. Encouraging them to plan for applying the actions or create triggers for when they'll apply their new skills can help make the commitment stick.

7. Check-In and Follow-Up

Sometime after the training event, create a check-in step. This can be as simple as an email asking learners to reflect on their progress over the last four to six weeks or a one-on-one meeting or phone call to discuss their challenges and successes. This uses the Return and Reflect Mode that we'll explore more in Step Four.

8. Refresh and Repeat

Create a way to refresh and repeat the training. This could be as simple as offering training alumni the chance to attend any future session, even if it's designed for beginners. You could create a pulse schedule where every three months or every year you engage the same group in the same topics while covering the same material, but you do fewer reviews on the algorithms and more discussion of the challenges. Ask the group to help each other solve their issues. It's rare for a one-and-done experience to stick. There is too much clamoring for our attention, and if we don't come back to key concepts over and over again, the brain will think the training is extraneous and delete it! Repetition works.

The Training Algorithm in Action

I want you to have an example of how this training algorithm can work in real life. Here's my secret sauce for my Accountability Activator workshop for leaders and managers:

Assign Pre-Work: Before the session, everyone answers a three-question email about their observations regarding good bosses and bad bosses.

Start with Mindset: We explore the Radical Candor™ mindset, getting them to think about their approach to being a boss and the "Jill version" of the Performance Values Matrix™. I also ask them to think about the people they're managing. When we finish the section, they acknowledge their goal of getting to the radical candor quadrant and spending more time with their people's top two quadrants.

Teach an Algorithm: I teach the Thinking Advantage algorithm of Teach, Coach, Don't Rescue, Return and Reflect, and a few additional algorithms (planned after assessing their pre-work needs and active issues).

Facilitate Practice: In between each algorithm, we do role-playing, where each person has the chance to be the boss while their partner is the employee. Then we switch! It's so fun to see bosses reacting as employees!

Discuss Challenges: We break into small groups and apply the algorithms to different scenarios that bosses see daily, bringing particularly sticky situations to the whole group for discussion and debate.

Encourage Commitment: At the end of the day, we reflect on the entire day, commit to three actions, and read them to a partner or the whole group.

Check-In and Follow-Up: Four weeks after the training day, attendees receive an email from me with three questions asking them to reflect on how they're doing with their commitments and what they've found useful or challenging.

Refresh and Repeat: All bosses continue to have access to Accountability Activator videos on my website (JillYoung.com/videos) to refresh their training. They use these videos during meetings or pull them into additional trainings. All bosses are invited and encouraged to keep attending the course for further understanding.

This is a simple formula to help you get the biggest bang for your buck, even if your buck is only one dollar. This algorithm is simple: You don't need it to be perfect for it to work.

You don't need perfect materials or a perfect location—there is never a perfect time to do training. You only need to start.

TRAINING THAT STICKS

1. ASSIGN PRE-WORK
2. START WITH MINDSET
3. TEACH AN ALGORITHM
4. FACILITATE PRACTICE
5. DISCUSS CHALLENGES
6. ENCOURAGE COMMITMENT
7. CHECK-IN AND FOLLOW-UP
8. REFRESH & REPEAT

Training also doesn't need to take a lot of time. The Parkinson Principle tells us that the task we're doing will expand to the time allotted. If you create space for two full days of training, you'll fill that space. If you only have two hours, you'll fill that space. I've had teams who created 30 minutes per week for training, and it worked! You have whatever time you allot.

The Theory of Constraints is also useful here. If we're constrained by time, we'll fill the time we do have with the *most important training*. One way I continue to assess the value of the training I deliver is if the leaders remark, "I wish we had more time." That means they're engaged with the topic. With adults, a little learning experience can go a long way. So, if they're hungry for more, they'll use the concepts and engage in reflection. And because adults learn best when there's an active issue (a working task to be done) and they learn best by doing, they can learn and be productive at the same time if we set up the training in the right time frame.

PRACTICAL APPLICATIONS

Here are some practical training applications that I've seen work in entrepreneurial companies:

Add Subject Matter Experts

Adding SME to someone's role in the Accountability Chart™ (a particularly formatted organizational chart used by companies running on EOS) spreads the accountability for expertise among the team rather than it resting only with the boss. SMEs are responsible for reading scholarly articles on their subjects, doing research, and diving into industry best, cutting edge practices. Then, they're responsible for bringing this knowledge to the company. This creates an environment where everyone teaches something.

Carefully Design the Week One Onboarding Experience

Leaders of companies who invest in training know that a first impression is critical for engaging people in learning. A great speaker or teacher starts a lesson with something funny, interesting, or engaging. Great companies create an engaging Week One experience for their new employees. Additionally, a great Week One empowers the rest of the training to have lots of self-direction and autonomy when done well. Think of it as giving trainees maps and formulas for great outcomes. I've found that great onboarding experiences include at least the following:

An Introduction to the Vision of the Company

If you run on EOS, you'll use your Vision/Traction Organizer™ to guide you through this part of onboarding. This sets the new employee up for success. It lets them know who we are, where we're going, and how we're going to get there. From day one, they'll know the big picture of the company. This could include the history of the company and stories of how the core values are used to hire, fire, review, reward, and recognize the people in the company. As a bonus, lots of great companies make it a point to have new employees meet with the top leaders of the company to hear parts of the vision. Other companies prioritize having the new employee learn the vision from others in the company and not only their manager. Still, other companies make sure they tie the vision-sharing to their culture with the way they onboard. If the culture is focused on achievement, the onboarding is done via a checklist. If the culture focuses on being open and honest, there is plenty of space for conversation vs. telling. If the culture is a lot of fun, the onboarding experience includes creating a nickname, a catchphrase, and a selfie with the head of the company. The bottom line is to make the vision stick, make the delivery memorable.

An Introduction and Overview of the Accountability Chart

Use a tool like the Accountability Chart, and within minutes, the new employee will see their role in the company's big picture and how they contribute to the vision. They'll also know who to go to if they have questions or need direction. They will see who they need to communicate with and who makes decisions on different company functions.

An Overview of the Processes They Need to Follow and Where to Find Them

Every company is different. If your company is running on EOS, you'll have your core processes documented, so they're easy to follow. During onboarding, your new employees must know where to find these processes, you go over what they'll be involved in, and invite any initial questions they have.

An Introduction and Overview of the Basic Tools of Their Role

This includes the software they'll use or the machines they'll operate. Even if they're the best accountants in the world and have 5,000 hours of QuickBooks experience, there are nuances, exceptions, and customizations your company has that they need to be aware of. If you've hired someone qualified for the job, they'll likely bring with them a "that's-how-I've-always-done-it" approach to their career. We owe it to them not to let them find out later that "that's not how we do it here." Be proactive in showing them how we do it here, even if it feels silly. It's better to find a missing link in their training now than to let it fester and create issues later.

An Overview of How They'll Be Measured

If you're running on EOS, this will be an overview of:

- The Meeting Pulse™: Tell them what meetings they're expected to attend, how to add issues to the Issues List, expectations for participation such as being on time and completing to-dos within seven days, how to call a Rock or Measurable on- or off-track, and an introduction to the Issues Solving Track™.

- Rocks: Explain the 90-Day World™ that you live in and your high priorities. This is a perfect time to agree on a few Rocks, or goals, for the remainder of the department's 90-day cycle.

- Measurables: Whether it's measured on a Scorecard or a general idea of how your company measures success on a daily basis, communicate the numerical way that you, as a boss, measure their success. Discuss being on the same page on this topic. How will you win the day? The week? The month? The year?

Establish a Pulse for Their First 90 Days

Somewhere in the first week, agree to the objectives (Rocks and Measurables) for an onboarding employee's first 90 days. Ideally, this includes how often they'll meet with their manager to reflect on what they're learning and answer their questions.

Pro Tip

Take advantage of what we know about timing and the order of events in a human experience. There is a lot of power in the order of how we experience events. In his book *When*, author Dan Pink states that we remember the beginning, the highlight, and the end of an experience. And in any experience, we usually have a lull or a slump in the middle. He advocates acknowledging that pattern and doing the boring or less engaging stuff in the middle of the experience.

I'm fully aware of the compliance and paperwork-related items that need to be communicated and filled out ASAP during onboarding a new employee. If you must do these in the first week, please don't let it be the very first thing they experience. Instead, put it in the middle somewhere. What if you start the onboarding with a bang by having someone welcome the new team member at the door on their first day or leave a gift package on their desk? What if you saved the compliance and paperwork for Wednesday afternoon and ended the week with a phone call from the CEO on Friday night asking how their first week went? Being thoughtful about the order rather than the agenda or checklist will help the Week One training stick.

Let Employees Be in Charge of Their Training

Just as I learned when I accidently discovered this method at the CPA firm, asking a team member to be in charge of their training progress is based on the adult learning principle of autonomy. This allows the learner a chance to proactively reach out to ask for help and get to know the people in the company in a real and purpose-driven way. This also takes the bulk of the training time off of the manager and puts it in the hands of the people doing the jobs. To implement this approach in your training plan, follow the guidelines below.

First, create the list:

- Ask the people doing the job to make a list of things a new employee needs to know. One way to say this is, "If I asked you to train a new employee, what would you teach them on their first day?" By using the phrase "their first day," you get straight to the essentials.

- Next, take that list to the department and ask the other people who interact with that position to add their items to the list.

- Lastly, from your point of view, add anything that is missing. This might include any compliance or government-required training as well.

Then, use the list:

- Ask the new employee to complete the training in a certain amount of time. Let her know that the SMEs will be expecting her to reach out to them to schedule a time to meet.

- Encourage the SMEs to ask the new employee to do some pre-work. If she is able to watch some videos, print off the processes, or locate some materials, the time spent with the SME will be more productive.

- Establish a time when she can ask you any questions or get clarity on things she's learning. Some bosses like to establish a daily pulse in the beginning. For example, make yourself available for your new employee every day from 10:00–10:30 a.m. This cuts down on multiple interruptions in your day and helps the new employee be organized and thoughtful with the time she has with you and the SMEs.

Give Someone Else Ownership of the Process

Like the SME, make ownership of processes something that shows up in the Accountability Chart. This works best when it isn't the boss who's accountable, but preferably someone doing the process daily. They become responsible for training and retraining people on the process, bringing process gaps to the team, updating the process with the team's solutions, and looking outside the organization for proactive process improvements.

Create a Video Library

Using videos to train has become increasingly effective and popular in the last five years. It's now common for companies to create a library of videos to help them train their people. I consistently produce training videos for my clients on a range of topics they add to their training libraries. If you've ever tried to explain a concept to someone and feel you aren't communicating it the same way you learned it or you end the conversation with, "Well, I guess you had to be there," you might consider adding videos to your company's training process. You can host these videos on YouTube or Vimeo or get serious and start using a Learning Management System (LMS).

Start Voluntary Book Clubs

Reading is one of the ways our brain processes and gathers information. With the ease of learning via audiobooks and videos, reading is becoming a lost art. Invite people in your company to join a book club with books that nudge them out of their comfort zones or reinforce business principles. Make discussion your focal point when you get together.

Form Mastermind Groups

Put together a group of people committed to learning together over an extended period. The group should consist of people who share similar roles and ambition levels. In 2017, I formed the Wise Woman Group of female business coaches who meet virtually on a regular schedule and once a year for a full weekend to learn from each other. Being connected to the same people, watching their journey, and coaching one another brings a deep level of learning I can't get if I only interact with someone once in a training setting.

Have a Top 10 List

This is an approach I use with companies when they feel pressed for time but want to train. It's a starting point that is a "progress, not perfection" approach (a term coined by Dan Sullivan), and it really sticks! To use this tool, ask the business expert to imagine that she only had one hour to teach someone how to do her job. What would she spend time teaching them? Ask that expert to start writing. Then, prioritize the topics. This becomes your top ten list, or in some cases, top eight or top thirteen. Use this as the basis for building a training session.

Establish a Company University

Several of the companies I coach have created an internal "university" that encapsulates a mix of the above ideas and has an accountable dean. The university has professors (SMEs) and a way for people to constantly add to it, Wikipedia-style. Key ingredients of successful internal universities are documented progression, partner or group teaching, simplicity, and fun.

WHAT WE'VE LEARNED

- The world of work has changed; constant training will help us stay adaptive and proactive.

- Training in the world of work needs to be focused on how adults learn.

- Training can come from everyone, not just the boss.

- Effective training can be simple; there is an algorithm to follow.

- Training doesn't need to take lots of time.

- If we don't invest in training as the first step in getting our people to think, the rest of the steps are frustrating and ineffective.

- When it comes to training, just start! There is never a perfect time to start, and *not* training is not an option.

Without teaching that sticks, the coaching we'll do in the next step is not time-effective. Leaders and managers can get bogged down with the coaching conversations they need to have. They'll take up unnecessary time, and both parties will end up frustrated. If this is how you've been feeling as you've tried to master being a great manager, could it be that you haven't invested time and energy into high-quality teaching?

POOR TEACHING IS THE CAUSE OF TIME CONSUMING COACHING. **EFFECTIVE TEACHING** ENABLES BRIEF, POWERFUL COACHING.

REFLECTION SECTION

1. What are you currently doing in your company to teach your people?

   _____

   _____

2. Now that you know how adults learn, what will you want to adjust in the training at your company?

   _____

   _____

3. What simple things can you change right now to be just one percent more effective?

   _____

   _____

4. What systemic changes will you discuss with your leadership team?

   _____

   _____

5. Whom have you identified that would benefit from more training?

   _____

   _____

6. How can you identify gaps in training?

   _____

   _____

STEP TWO
COACH

 TEACH

 COACH

 DON'T RESCUE

 RETURN& REFLECT

Imagine you've trained Paul. He's about 90 days into his new job and is finishing up his training checklist. He has built good relationships with his coworkers and is on track to be a very productive member of the team. This morning he got stuck while working on a project. He's not sure what to do next; he's feeling some tension and starts to think, *Where can I get an answer?*

You pop into his mind because you told him if he's ever stuck to come see you, so he comes to your office and says, "Hey, boss. I'm stuck. What button do I push, the red one or the green one?" and you say, "The green one." He hustles back to his office totally satisfied.

It worked! You got him unstuck, and you both got back to work. This is beautiful! You feel like a great boss, and he feels like a great employee. Neither one of you has any tension left, and you've gone back to a state of satisfaction. You both feel good. That good feeling is desirable, so you both think, "Great! We'll do that again next time we find ourselves in this situation!"

This happens over and over again: Paul comes to your office with questions, and you give answers. Both of you high-five and feel amazing about your teamwork. In isolation, this doesn't seem so bad, but in a growing company with big goals, it's at the heart of what will hold that company back.

If you have eight direct reports, you might play this scenario out 20 or more times per day with each interaction taking a toll on your completion of higher-order leadership tasks. Each time you're interrupted, it takes time to get back to what you were working on. When you aren't available, work halts until your employee gets an answer from you, creating a bottleneck. The bottleneck is at the top of the bottle, and you've created it.

WHAT IS COACHING?

I've had lots of training and read lots of books on coaching. It's a good thing, because I'm a coach and help people see and live life differently. I help them see what they can't see themselves and get to the heart of their issues so they can solve them. All of this is what a coach does.

Boiling it down to its essence, I define coaching simply as helping people become their best. When we train people, it helps them get started and learn how to do the task. Coaching is helping people become their very best at that task or in their role. This is the step where we'll start to stretch their understanding of what they were trained on. We'll really fire up the thinking part of the brain!

COACHING IS...
HELPING PEOPLE BECOME
THEIR BEST

When I was trained as an EOS Implementer, before I arrived at Boot Camp, I was asked to prepare a rough draft of my entrepreneurial story, compile a list of my entrepreneurial contacts, and watch several videos (that's an example of pre-work in action). Little did I know that I'd go back to those videos so often.

When I had a question or got confused about one of the tools, my coach told me, "Go watch the video." EOS Worldwide knows that 80% of the questions that new EOS Implementers have will come up time and time again. Since there is so much to absorb to be an effective EOS Implementer, and to eliminate some of the burden on the coaches, EOS Worldwide had the foresight to create training videos.

Can you imagine the coaching that would need to happen if the training system were not in place? When I had a question or scenario that wasn't covered in a video, my coach engaged in coaching and helped me think through the situation, shared stories of when they'd been in the same scenario, and shared what worked or didn't work for them. Sometimes, I posed questions like this to the whole community and got four or five things I could consider to solve my issue.

Here's the point: Training should cover the basics and the foundations and should be repeatable in an effortless way. ("Go watch the videos.") Coaching, on the other hand, explores the exceptions, the deeper thinking, and the application of current principles to new ideas and unique circumstances. It helps people become their best and improve on the basics.

IF TRAINING IS THE SCIENCE... ...COACHING IS THE ART.

Coaching can be a part of leadership and management, but it's only one skill you'll want to have as a leader and a manager. Consider this: To be a coach, you don't need to be a leader or a manager. You don't need an official management or leadership role to coach. Sometimes, coaching is more effective when there isn't an authoritative relationship. In his second book, *Death of the Org Chart*, Walt Brown argues that our thinking and learning relationships, "those that center around reporting, mentoring and coaching, must be overt, in the open, clearly spelled out, communicated and adjusted for individuals to grow inside their organization." Ideally, everyone in the company would have a manager *and* a coach. Heck, every human should have a coach! How beneficial would it be to our world if everyone had someone who added energy to them and encouraged them to be their best? Keep this in mind in the following sections as *you* learn how to be a coach.

HOW BENEFICIAL WOULD IT BE TO OUR WORLD IF EVERYONE HAD SOMEONE WHO ADDED ENERGY TO THEM, ENCOURAGING THEM TO BE THEIR BEST?

Dan Sullivan, cofounder of The Strategic Coach™ Program and coach to over 20,000 entrepreneurs over 40 years states, "Coaching is the number one skill of the 21st century." He claims that the power of coaching is more useful than ever because the world has become very complex. We now have access to more communication, more ideas, more choices, more opinions, more data, and more inaccuracies in that data. When we have complexity in our lives, our brains have a hard time sorting through the data and separating the signals from the noise. Coaching simplifies this.

Think about a time when you experienced coaching. This could be during participation in a sports team or debate team, while meeting with your financial planner, through life coaching, or anytime you went to someone you trusted to work through a problem. If you're running on EOS, you've experienced coaching during your sessions with your Implementer!

What did you experience?

_____

_____

_____

_____

Here is what I've experienced as I've been coached (Yes! Coaches need coaches.) and what many others report experiencing:

- *An aha moment*: This is when you feel that lightbulb turn on. You suddenly see things in a new way or you have a new idea.

- *Getting unstuck*: Before the coaching, you were stuck; you couldn't see a path forward. After the coaching, you see a path forward.

- *Clarity*: This is the feeling of having a muddy water brain become clear: before, lots of variables, scenarios, and what-ifs are floating around in your mind. When you experience coaching around these topics, things become clear. Coaching helps the mud settle so you're left with clear water.

- *Creativity*: When two or more people are engaged in coaching, the Mastermind Effect is present. The power of two heads are better than one, and many times, it results in greater amounts of or higher-quality creativity.

- *Confidence*: The experience of coaching brings confidence to both the coach and the coached. Sometimes, all we need to move forward and be our best is simply the confidence to act.

How much more effective could your company be if everyone in the company were having more of these experiences on a daily basis? Would it seem almost magical?

Rich Litvin, one of the universe's most effective and sought-after coaches says, "Coaching is not magic, but it can seem magical in its impact." If you're reading this book, it's highly likely that you've coached people, maybe not even realizing you're doing it! To help you see what kind of tendencies you have as a coach, we'll use a mindset—a mental model that helps you think about coaching in a new way.

THE COACHING MAGIC MATRIX

In this matrix, we start with two concepts of how you're thinking about the people you're coaching. In this model, we'll focus on how we coach direct reports. Remember, this can apply to coaching all types of people: kids, vendors, trade partners, third party vendors, peers, and even clients!

The way you're *thinking* tends to influence the way you act or what approach you take. So, let's start with two ways of thinking.

Short-term or Long-term Thinking

Short-term thinking about your people sounds like this:

- I want my employees to be happy working here.

- I like it when they refer their friends.

- I want them to have fun and be excited to come to work every day!

- It's faster to do it myself than teach her to do it.

- This new issue that came up today needs to be solved right now.

- I don't want to hurt their feelings.

- I'm afraid they might quit if I put too much pressure on them.

Long-term thinking about your people sounds like this:

- I want my people to flourish.

- I want them to have rich experiences while working here that will deepen their purpose and enrich their entire lives.

- I want my people to feel challenged; it will make them stronger.

- I want them to have opportunities for success and failure.

- I really want my people to grow, love growing, and be deeply invested in helping one another and our clients grow.

The second concept that is a key ingredient in your coaching approach is how you think about your employees' *abilities* and *potential*. Do you think about them from a deficit- or possibility-based perspective?

Deficit- or Possibility-based Thinking

A deficit thinker sounds like this:

- Well, you can't teach an old dog new tricks!

- It's easier to do it myself than to teach her how to do it.

- It takes a long time for people to be productive and really contribute.

- I must be on that client's account; they won't work with anyone but me.

- I'm afraid that no one will ever be able to replace me.

A possibility thinker sounds like this:

- I wonder what ideas our new people have for solving this problem.

- Let's get Susan into a peer group to help her grow.

- Who else could teach this class?

- We have so much talent in our company. Who needs more responsibility?

- Who can I spend time with to encourage them?

We are now set up to examine what happens when you *combine* these two spectrums of thinking (or mindsets). Keep in mind the lessons we learned about using a mental model to teach (hint: I'm about to do that right now!) and how it helps people think about their thinking as well as individualize the teaching to their lives.

This isn't meant to put a forever label on someone. The intention is to observe the world from a new or bigger perspective. Here we go!

The Professor Approach

When you have long-term thinking combined with deficit-based thinking, I call that the professor approach. You teach and teach and teach. You think your direct report needs to know more, learn more, or give it more time. Your first thought in managing is that the person needs more training. You rely on your processes to get the work done. If it's in the process, people can't make mistakes. If people follow the process, they'll get results. You expect perfection; you think utopia is possible. You're frustrated by being the only one who knows things but don't see a way out of it. You hope the training pays off someday and are constantly updating and creating more processes. You long for the day when you aren't the only one people come to for answers. You usually have a long line of people asking for answers. Sometimes people see you as a know-it-all.

The Buddy Approach

When you have short-term thinking combined with deficit-based thinking, I call that the buddy approach. You want your people to like you and to have a great time at work. Because of this, you offer to help with lots of projects. Your door is always open, and you often spend more time at work than others trying to get all of your to-dos done. You're busy and take pride in knowing you're highly productive and get stuff done. You don't want to push your people too hard; they might quit, and it's a pain to replace people. So you're willing to overlook mistakes or lack of effort. You take on extra work because you think you're the only one who can do it. It's hard to think about the company without your involvement. The buck stops with you *a lot*. You take monkeys (I'll explain this later)! It wouldn't work otherwise. Sometimes, you feel that your people take you for granted.

The Cheerleader Approach

When you have short-term combined with possibility-based thinking, you tend to take the cheerleader approach. People love to be around you because of your positive attitude. You're an encourager and a supporter, the one to pump people up. You give lots of praise and make things exciting. You know we can do anything we set our minds to! When things don't live up to your expectations, you justify it, make excuses, and ask people to try harder next time. Sometimes, issues are left unresolved; you hope they'll go away on their own. If you're gone from the office too long, productivity goes up (and that seems weird to you), but morale starts to wane because you've created a dependency on your motivation.

The Coach Approach

When you have long-term thinking combined with possibility-based thinking, I call that the coach approach. You are authentic, just as comfortable sharing stories about your strengths and successes as you are about your weaknesses and failures. You aren't the guru and rarely claim to have all the answers. Yet people deeply value their conversations with you. When they leave the conversation, they feel both heard and motivated to act. You regularly have conversations that most people would call difficult, but you enter them and exit them with a humble confidence that you've built by being real with people. You're truly curious and care about getting to the heart of the issue, and you are patient in doing so. You value coaching because you, too, seek coaching from others. Many people you coach go on to coach others.

REFLECTION SECTION

1. In which quadrant do you see yourself thinking most of the time?

   _____

   _____

2. What examples can you think of that would give evidence of living in this quadrant?

   _____

   _____

3. Do you ever find yourself in the coach approach quadrant? If so, when?

   _____

   _____

For me, I was able to create a lot of success with the cheerleader approach. I distinctly remember driving to work each day back in my 20s when I was managing childcare centers. As soon as I'd get a few blocks from the center, a slight feeling of dread would begin to build in the pit of my stomach. I felt pressure to be positive, happy, and a light for the rest of the center, yet I knew there'd be issues to solve once I arrived because that's how the business was. It had humans in it, and therefore, there were issues. At that time, I didn't have an operating system, a leadership team, or a coach. The way I coped with that stress was to smile more and give my people whatever they asked for.

It wasn't until early in my coaching practice that I learned about healthy conflict, truly serving people instead of simply pleasing them, and making decisions with the long-term, greater good of the company in mind. As I've grown and have had the chance to practice the art of coaching every day, I live more in the coach approach than I used to, but I still observe myself in the other quadrants often.

My goal is to get you living at least one percent more in the coach quadrant, and for that, I have an algorithm called Coaching Magic!

If this is feeling a bit like the movie *Inception*, I apologize. Yes, this is an algorithm *within* an algorithm!

OBSERVE MODE

FOUR MODES OF COACHING MAGIC

1. OBSERVE
2. RESPOND
3. CO-CREATE
4. RETURN & REFLECT

When you proactively look for opportunities to help and serve others, you add your energy to their growth. Observing means actively looking for moments when someone has a chance to think!

Observing involves engaging with reality and looking for the truth, both positive and negative. It involves noticing and accepting where the person is, what they're thinking, and how they're behaving. It's a very simple act that some leaders find difficult to do because we tend to rush to judgment. In this step, you observe the truth of the situation. Dan Sullivan says, "All progress starts with telling the truth." Observing is a way to witness reality: what the truth is in this moment.

Leaders who regularly use Observe Mode to its fullest have found that they do it best when their mind is clear. They report taking time for self-care, stepping away from the day-to-day busyness and taking regular Clarity Breaks™.

A Clarity Break is a tool taught in the EOS Toolbox™ that helps a leader gain clarity on the big issues and create a calm mind for herself. As with all EOS Tools, it's simple, real, and gets results. To take a Clarity Break, first schedule 60–120 minutes with yourself on your calendar. Block it off and treat it as an important meeting with yourself. The *most* important person who needs clarity in the business is the boss. We're all following you, so you must be clear on where we're headed or on the issue at hand.

During this time that you've scheduled for yourself, go to a place where you won't be distracted. Actively protect your attention by turning off all electronics, notifications, and ringers! Then, simply sit with a blank legal pad and think. That's it! There is no more to this tool than giving yourself time to think. Think about what? You decide. Your brain only needs a calm, distraction-free space to let you know what's important.

If you still need to be sold on the power of a Clarity Break, consider this: Do you ever have ideas in the middle of the night, while you're in the shower, or while you're driving somewhere? Do you wake up with ideas or suddenly remember something as you sit down to relax? Most busy leaders shout "Yes!" when I ask this question. This happens because, in all these scenarios (sleeping, showering, driving), your brain slows down to almost a hypnotic pace. (I know, we should stay totally alert while driving, but this is the truth.

For most of us, driving has become automatic rather than an active mental state.)

There is so much that your brain is trying to tell you and so many thoughts backed up and bottlenecked because of your constant activity that when the logical, active frontal cortex starts to slow down, the subconscious, deep-thinking part of your brain finally has a chance to surface, offering you clarity or showing ideas you wouldn't usually pay attention to. Leaders who engage in some kind of slowing-down time will find that observing truth becomes easier. They can listen with their eyes, use their feelings as a barometer, and coach their people effectively (more on those observation techniques below).

OBSERVE VS. IGNORE

The opposite of *observe* is *ignore*. During one of my first sessions with a new client, we were reviewing and modifying the Accountability Chart and getting it ready to roll out. A leader asked the question, "In the operations leader seat that I sit in, there are three letters at the top: LMA™. What does LMA stand for?"

I answered, "In EOS, LMA stands for *lead*, *manage*, and *hold accountable*."

"Oh," he said. "I thought it stood for *leave me alone*."

Although we enjoyed a good laugh, this is sometimes the attitude bosses take. They ignore their people and send a signal that says *leave me alone*. And it's easy to do! There are skeletons in the closet that are easier to ignore than to deal with and issues that are easier to sweep under the rug than to work on and solve.

Have you ever had an experience similar to this? Keith, a top leader with a growing company, called me one afternoon for some coaching with a sticky situation. He reported that he thought his sales leader, Stacy, wasn't in the right seat. As he shared some data and examples of what he'd observed, he said, "I wish I had seen this sooner."

When he said that, I asked him, "When did you know? Looking back on the past year, when did you really know that she wasn't right for the seat?"

After some silence and thinking out loud, Keith figured he really knew about eight months before, but he ignored the signs and the early indicators that something was off. If he'd observed and examined the truth about those early indicators, he could have had a conversation earlier and possibly coached Stacy toward success in her role.

In Observe Mode, one phrase I often use is "Easy now, hard later. Hard now, easy later." When we observe and subsequently take care of the hard issues now, life becomes easier in the long run. When we ignore the signs and take the easy way out now, life becomes hard in the long term and the issue often compounds itself, becoming very complex and messy.

Keith learned that living in Observe Mode takes daily energy and constant vigilance to gather observations and help people become their best. This is also reality. If we want something to grow and thrive, we must add energy consistently. Think of a simple plant. We know that if we add the right amounts of high-quality water, light, and soil, the plant will grow. If we take those things away or are inconsistent with those sources of energy, the plant shrivels and eventually dies.

Our people are no different. I've heard people in leadership positions ruminate or complain that they shouldn't need to motivate their people constantly. They shouldn't need to remind people of the vision or core values so often. This is simply arguing with reality. If adding energy to your people and their growth is something you don't want to do or don't enjoy doing, please don't take leadership positions. Do something else with your talent. The book *How to Be a Great Boss* by Gino Wickman and René Boer states, "If you do not love people, don't be a boss."

Here's the great news! You may already have systems in place that help direct your observations. They may be right in front of you, just underutilized in your coach approach. If you run on EOS, the EOS Foundational Tools™ alone are a perfect place to start:

- **The Accountability Chart** holds the five roles that each seat is accountable for. Observe regularly if your people own these responsibilities.

- **Rocks** are agreed-to 90-day priorities. Everyone in the company has one to three Rocks every 90 days. Observe regularly if these Rocks are getting done and if they're on- or off-track during the 90 days.

- **Scorecards** track the most important numbers weekly, allowing you to regularly observe the results of agreed-upon outcomes. Observe if the numbers they're responsible for on the Scorecard are usually hit or missed.

- **Meeting Pulse** allows you to meet with your team at the right time, for the right duration, and with the right agenda, giving everyone the chance to stay on the same page and be accountable to each other. Observe if your team members are engaged in issues-solving and responsible to last week's to-dos.

- **The Vision/Traction Organizer** is a two-page document that holds the answers to eight basic questions that form your Vision. It is the guide for decision-making and culture. Observe if your direct report is in alignment with this V/TO™ or is wavering in some way.

Using these tools or similar approaches will help keep your observations focused on meaty issues and create productive conversations and collaborations in the future.

OBSERVE LIKE A PRO

Listen with Your Eyes

All too often, we rely on words alone to communicate. Similarly, though we trust that the words other people say are true, the reality is that the words people use aren't always clear or reflective of what's going on. I'm not talking about flat-out lying; it's more subtle than that. Humans have an innate need or instinct to protect ourselves, *and* we've mastered our languages, sometimes creating 100 words for the same object, feeling, etc. (If you want to do a fun exercise, create two teams and have one team find synonyms for the word *big* and the other team find synonyms for the word *little*. You'll be surprised how many they'll come up with!) Because of this, words sometimes hide the real story.

One way to get to more of the truth is to listen with your eyes. This means watching the body language of others and inquiring when the words and body language seem incongruent. Michael Allosso's *You on Your Best Day* calls these micro-messages. If we aren't proactively in Observe Mode, we'll miss these micro-messages, and our brains will get confused.

I listen with my eyes regularly when I'm in sessions with leadership teams. During one preparation call with the leader of a manufacturing company, the leader said he wanted his team to be engaged in the planning of the vision of the company. Yet, during the session, I observed that when his team spoke, he rarely reflected on their ideas or contributions, his body language appeared tired, and he didn't make eye contact.

Though his words expressed his desire to have them involved, the micro-messaging in his actions was incongruent.

When I inquired about this further, his real thoughts weren't about re-engaging his team but how to re-engage himself with the vision. He'd grown disillusioned over the years.

Another example: In the middle of a session with a long-term client, I noticed one of the leadership team members was unusually quiet, so I asked him his thoughts on the topic. At the break, a woman on the team pulled me aside and commented, "You watch everything. You seem to know exactly when someone isn't saying what they want to say. How do you do that?" The secret is observing the micro-messages!

Use Your Feelings as a Barometer

It is a myth that a coach, facilitator, or boss must stay neutral and can't take sides. If you've approached your work with this thought, one thing you might be missing is how to use your feelings as an observation tool. Sometimes, we try to approach situations with a neutral mindset (a forced and unnatural state, just as perfect balance is unnatural). We need tension and relief, push and pull, ups and downs to keep the momentum in life and business going. I encourage you to let go of neutrality to allow yourself to feel your way into Observe Mode.

Lest you think I'm advocating for leading or coaching with only feelings or subjectivity, I'm not. I'm encouraging you to use your feelings as a data point. Allow them to help you feel when something may be going on that you can't see in the data or hear in your team's words.

In the same way I listen with my eyes, I use my feelings when I'm in the Observe Mode of coaching. After a tension-filled argument between a father and son on a leadership team of seven, I said to the team, "Well, that was uncomfortable for me to coach the two of you through. Is anyone else feeling the same way?" On the surface, one might feel I'd lose my credibility as a facilitator by admitting to that discomfort. People on the team could think facilitators should expect some uncomfortable moments and learn ways how not to be uncomfortable. But in reality, I still feel that way, and other people in the room feel that way. I'm not going to argue with reality, because when I do, I always lose! In acknowledging my feelings, I allow others to acknowledge their feelings.

In this particular situation, the team discussed how the father and son's public arguments had caused a rift in the company's culture, making many people question the company's future viability under the son's eventual ownership. Because I used my feelings as a barometer and asked if anyone else felt the same way, we got to the root of an issue faster than we would have using facts-and-figures data.

Feelings are a data point. Use them as a signal that something isn't being said, something is funky, or that there are issues we need to look into or aren't seeing. *Important note: I don't use my feelings to find the answer or solution. I use my feelings to ask questions.*

REFLECTION SECTION

1. What structures or tools do you already have in place to help you observe?

   _____

   _____

2. What are you observing now that you used to ignore?

   _____

   _____

3. Think about a time when you thought (as Keith did above on page 51) _I wish I had seen this sooner._ In hindsight, what were you observing that you didn't acknowledge?

   _____

   _____

   _____

   _____

4. Is there anything you are observing now that you'd like to solve? What is your next step with this?

   _____

   _____

   _____

   _____

RESPOND MODE

FOUR MODES OF COACHING MAGIC

1 OBSERVE
2 RESPOND
3 CO-CREATE
4 RETURN & REFLECT

In this step of the algorithm, you choose to respond by thinking about your thinking and helping others do the same. The opposite of responding is mindless and thoughtless reaction. The healthier choice is to respond.

My introduction to the concept that individuals can and should choose their response was when I read *Man's Search for Meaning* by Viktor E. Frankl. In this powerful yet painful book, Frankl lets us into his world and his thinking and we discover what kept him alive during his time as a prisoner in a Nazi concentration camp. Frankl taught this formula: event plus response equals outcome.

$$E + R = O$$

Events will happen, and in life, we rarely have control over events that happen to us or around us. What we do have control over is our response. You can't control that an employee isn't accountable, but you can control your response to it. You can't control the outcome, yet your response to the event can affect the outcome. When your response is focused on the long term and fueled by possibility-based thinking, you will have the best chance for a positive outcome.

CHOOSING YOUR RESPONSE

Choose Your Response...

INVITE THINKING WITH

- curiosity
- the greater good
- optimism
- gratitude
- taking responsibility

REPEL THINKING WITH

- avoidance, denial
- anger
- disappointment
- inflexibility
- guilt, blame, shame

It would be a wonderful, utopian world if we were allotted ample time to choose our response to any event intentionally. During the emergency water landing in the Hudson River in 2009, many people questioned the decisions of Captain Chesley "Sully" Sullenburger when he chose the response of landing his plane in the Hudson River.

When the data was examined at the subsequent FAA hearing, several experts observed that he could have and should have turned the plane around to land safely at an airport. Captain Sully testified that response time hadn't been added to the simulations the experts had run. It took the Captain and his ground team a full 55 seconds to process the information and decide. If this case seems extreme, it's because lives were at stake. In the real world, sometimes 55 seconds is a luxury in which to choose our response.

I imagine that if we did live in that utopian world where we could push pause on everything while we chose our response, we'd have more peace and happiness among the humans inhabiting our planet. We are social beings who are often irrational and instinct driven. Other people's behavior affects ours, and sometimes, their plans or actions don't coincide with our desired timing.

Because of this, people like you and me strive to live in the coach approach and pre-think and rehearse our responses. Our intention is to be ready to engage in coaching at any time, just as Captain Sully's practice in the simulator allowed him to protect every life on his aircraft.

Some Respond Approaches

Here are some possibility-based and long-term focused Respond approaches that get favorable outcomes. (This list isn't exhaustive but a good start. Feel free to come up with your own.)

Curiosity

When we take a curious approach in our response, we withhold judgment. This allows us to really listen and seek to understand the person we're coaching.

Compassion

Choosing to respond with compassion involves simply *being* with a person in their thoughts. The goal of the compassion response is to help this person feel heard and acknowledge their feelings are normal.

For the Greater Good

When we take the "for the greater good" approach, we think of a bigger picture; we think long term. We rise above the situation to focus on what's really important. We think about the outcome we'd like to see instead of the immediate issue in front of us. We choose to enter into the hard topics now to allow us an easier future.

Optimism

Choosing to respond with optimism involves going into situations knowing for certain there is a solution. We take a "How can we …?" position with issues because we know there are many paths to getting to the solution or goal.

Gratitude

Choosing this response requires showing appreciation for the person, the issue, or the situation itself. Responding with gratitude involves acknowledging people for the work they've already done or thought they were doing. It can also be useful when someone brings a big issue to light that would otherwise be hidden. When you choose to be appreciative, people are more likely to speak freely and get to the real issue more quickly.

Take Responsibility

Taking responsibility for your actions or the actions of the company or event shows humility. When you own the responsibility for the outcome, you show strength and leadership. When you practice using apologies with this approach, you strengthen the human connection.

Some React Approaches

Here are some deficit-thinking based and short-term focused "react" approaches that get unfavorable outcomes. (Again, not an exhaustive list. Feel free to add things to this list as you find new strategies that don't work for you.)

Avoidance

Doing nothing is an active, chosen response. It's the most prevalent response for coaches who fall into the buddy approach quadrant, depending on how often it's chosen. Be careful—avoidance can be disguised as a wait-and-see approach or an information gathering phase.

Never before in my coaching history had I witnessed the effects of this more than in the spring of 2020, as the threat to our global economy became very real for me and my clients. Suddenly, we met in an emergency zombie apocalypse mode. Some of the teams needed to lay off people and restructure their company seats and roles to stabilize the companies' futures. As we reflected on who would be on the furlough or lay-off lists, most managers admitted (or finally became aware) they'd been avoiding handling their people issues because they hadn't been such a big deal before this moment. When I asked the question, "Which of your current people will you absolutely need to rebuild?" and conversely, "Who would you not hire back?" we uncovered a previous avoidance and lack of response to issues.

What I learned for myself, even though I knew it in theory, is that critical issues need to be solved in times of peace to achieve the long-term vision. When we're in times of crisis, these issues come to the forefront in a very real way.

Anger

When we choose (or react with) anger, our brains are cut off from any study, preparation, or logical plans on which we'd previously relied. Because we're human, I'm sure you can see yourself in some of these examples:

- *With my teenagers*: "I'm so sick of you spending all of your money on fast food. It's so irresponsible. You're a smart person. Why would you do something so stupid? Now you'll never have enough money to buy a car." As painful as this is to admit, I heard myself say these words a few years ago after my first teenager started working.

- *With employees*: "I can't believe you have the nerve to ask for a raise. I've already done so much for you. It seems that all you care about is money."

- *With vendors*: "This is unacceptable. You promised that the product would be delivered by now. If this is how your company operates, you can rest assured that all of my colleagues will be hearing about how you never follow through on what you promised."

When I'm in active Return and Reflect Mode with leaders who have reacted with anger, they report feeling disappointed in themselves. After we react with anger, these are very common reflections. I hear them all the time.

1. "I am disappointed in my reaction. It was uncalled for. I wish I could take it back."

2. "That was a stupid thing to say. I don't even feel that way."

3. "After thinking about the words I chose, I realize they are inaccurate."

4. "I didn't even recognize myself. It's like I had an out-of-body experience, almost like watching myself explode."

Here's why these statements are true, in a biological sense. When we're angry, our brains are flooded with cortisol. Cortisol is sort of a built-in alarm system. It helps us prioritize protecting our physical selves and our egoic selves.

Suppose we've been wronged or disappointed in a situation or outcome and we react with anger—we rarely reflect on the truth because some of the truth may reflect negatively on our behavior.

Furthermore, we use extreme language to solidify our position of being the victim in the situation. For example, if I'd been truthful in my anger with my teenager and said the truth—that he only spent 58% of his money on fast food—it would have weakened my second argument—"You'll never be able to save money for a new car." That would put my ego at risk. So my brain took over and enhanced my argument by using extreme language.

Disappointment

Reacting with disappointment happens when an initial expectation or agreement is broken. If you really had a clear agreement, it's natural to feel disappointed, and you can sit with that. Taking the approach of disappointment, though, demonstrates traits found in the professor approach quadrant of our table. The professor is disappointed in the student rather than choosing to see the failure as a learning opportunity. When we choose to take the "I'm very disappointed in you and your behavior; I expected more from you" approach, it most often leads to a deficit-thinking and short-term focused reaction from the person we're coaching. This inevitably results in a downward spiral toward a less productive outcome.

Inflexibility

If you've attached yourself to a way of thinking that doesn't allow for creativity or other paths, your response will rarely be beneficial. Inflexible thinking is a quick way to unhappiness—you have a goal and believe there is only one path to get to that goal. Think outside your box.

Denial or Arguing with Reality

On her website *TheWork.com*, Byron Katie says that there are only three kinds of business: (1) My business, (2) Other people's business, and (3) God's business. She states that God's business is anything that is basic reality. When we deny reality, we're messing with God's business. Being in denial of reality rarely leads to calm, clear, and possibility-based thinking. I can only control my business and my state of mind.

Fear

A few years ago, I was talking with a man who considered hiring me to be the business coach for his leadership team. We were having a pleasant conversation, then it quickly turned deep. He said, "Jill, I know full well how using you as our coach will work. Can you talk to me about when it may not work?" The question had never been posed to me quite so clearly. We explored past situations in which my coaching hasn't had a positive effect and discussed a few reasons why this happens.

After the call ended, I thought so long and hard about this question that I wrote a whole book on it called *The Courage Advantage*. What I discovered in my research for that book and after observing leadership teams in over 500 sessions was that some teams embraced the coaching and systems and other teams fizzled out or couldn't make the system work within their organizations. All of the teams received the same coaching and had access to the same tools, but the big difference was the teams who didn't make it let fear guide their companies.

If you choose the fear response, you might hear yourself starting your sentences with the phrase "I'm afraid that …" It's something I now listen for from leaders—and then I challenge their fears (fear of what others will think, fear of loss, fear of making a mistake, etc.). Some leaders have chosen the fear response for so long, they don't even notice it.

Guilt

About a decade ago, I was in church when the teacher explained the three reasons people obey. (In that context, the discussion was about obeying God, but I think it applies to more than that.) The first reason is out of fear. They fear the consequences if they don't obey. The second is out of duty. They feel a responsibility to obey. And the third is they obey out of love. They feel intrinsic reward and satisfaction because they really love God or the person asking for obedience. When we choose the response of guilt, it's akin to obeying out of duty.

I recently enjoyed a workout at my regular gym when I saw a friend of mine also working out. Because she practiced the same religion, she quickly explained how guilty she felt for working out on a Sunday (something not normally acceptable in our culture). To justify it, she exclaimed that she wasn't even wearing her heart monitor that would record the "offense," and therefore, she wouldn't receive credit for the workout.

After class, I inquired a bit further into her feelings. She mentioned that guilt was her number one motivator for action. She shared with me that guilt worked for her, and she was conscious that she was using it often as her chosen and even unchosen reaction to events in her life.

As a business leader, you'll make mistakes, forget things, and often make wrong decisions. There are plenty of chances to feel guilty, but staying in that feeling and responding with that feeling won't serve you in the long term. You'll be much better served by taking responsibility and moving on.

Blame and Shame

This is similar to guilt, but it involves trying to place that feeling of guilt on another person instead of yourself. Choosing a response of blame and shame can entice the other person or people in the interaction to obey, or cooperate, out of fear and guilt. The higher order choice is love, joy, purpose, etc. However, this blame and shame response works so well that its powerful, immediate outcome sometimes reinforces it. However, at its core, this response eats away at everyone's confidence in the interaction or conversation.

Choose Your Response...

INVITE THINKING WITH
- curiosity
- the greater good
- optimism
- gratitude
- taking responsibility

REPEL THINKING WITH
- avoidance, denial
- anger
- disappointment
- inflexibility
- guilt, blame, shame

When we intentionally choose to respond in a way that is possibility-based and long-term focused, we start using one of the most effective teaching tools of our species: the power of leading by example. The way you choose to approach coaching is as important as the solution you co-create with your people. A healthy approach will help you choose a response that'll serve you for the long term. As a leader, it isn't your job to deliver a message; you *are* the message. How you respond affects how your employees will respond.

In this next section, you'll learn some ways to choose your response. The more you practice, the better you'll get.

INITIATING THE COACHING CONVERSATION

MAGIC HAPPENS
INSIDE
THE CONVERSATION

Magic happens *inside* the conversation. Conversations, when structured well, get to the heart of real issues. I've observed that bosses spend more time worrying about *possible* outcomes of a conversation than they spend conversing with their people. Although I love the concept of deliberate practice, worrying is not considered practice. Neither are good intentions.

In the summer of 2018, I decided that I wanted to start playing the piano again. Because I know the concept of deliberate practice, I bought sheet music, researched the best keyboards, set a practice schedule, and set up the space to be exciting and rewarding. After a few practice sessions, I got off track and worried I wouldn't meet my new goal. I rearranged the area, bought different (easier) sheet music, and adjusted the practice schedule. None of that worked or counted toward practicing the instrument. The only thing that worked was putting my fingers on the keyboard and spending time with the piano and the music.

I see this same thing happen with leaders. They spend time reading articles and books, attending trainings, asking others for advice, and worrying, journaling about, meditating on, and praying about their people and their people issues. But none of these counts toward the practice of having great coaching conversations. The only thing that helps you become a better coach is to coach!

The medium that coaches use is conversations. Nothing magical happens outside the conversation. I've also noticed that leaders fear having conversations because they might elicit an undesirable reaction or response from their team members. This fear isn't unfounded. Every individual gets to choose their response. They may react harshly, but that is their choice, not yours. Easier said than done, right? I hear you! So, I have a gift for you—an unlimited, all-access season pass of do-overs.

UNLIMITED DO-OVERS

As I've grown as a coach, I've certainly messed up and said things that triggered responses of fear, guilt, shame, or resentment. In one particular situation, I took a bold approach with a leadership team member who was sensitive to public coaching. Unaware of the situation (I wasn't observing at a coach level), I continued to ask probing questions that held him accountable for his results and offered him a different approach, all within about one minute. I was doing all the talking and focused more on my checklist than on him. About a week later, the business owner called me and reported that this leader was anxious and worried and didn't feel like being in the room with me. Ugh, that hurt. Although I followed a process that'd worked a hundred times before, I fell into a pattern of checking my list vs. connecting and coaching deeply.

Here's something positive I'd like to offer as a takeaway from this painful story: I apologized. A few days later, I had a conversation with the team member, admitted that I had not been the best coach in that moment, and asked for a do-over. Our relationship is now deeper and better *because* I messed up! So, feel free to mess up as you're coaching, and be ready to apologize. The apology connects and creates a shared accomplishment.

You now have unlimited use of this season pass of do-overs! Knowing this will help you jump into a conversation without the requirement of perfection. It'll help you start coaching.

Back to the step at hand: Initiating the coaching conversation. I've observed that there are two primary ways to engage in this step. The first way is when someone comes to you. They initiate the conversation.

When They Come to You

The fastest way from point A to point B is a straight line, and you are your team's straight line. By default, you're the fastest and easiest way for them to get an answer. And while you want to make time for them, the goal is for them to need you less—not as much for direction and more for support and critical thinking collaboration. Humans love things to be easy. We find the path of least resistance, the least painful path that involves less energy and work. We do this because we're human, not because we're lazy or disengaged. We're biologically designed to conserve energy, and thinking expends energy. So, if we think we can pop into our boss's office and ask a quick question and get a quick answer, we'll try that first. Our brain knows this is the path to spend the least amount of energy. When your people come to you, getting an answer is their main priority. From now on, when your people come to you, your main priority is to engage them in *thinking*.

WHEN YOUR PEOPLE COME TO YOU, YOUR MAIN PRIORITY IS TO ENGAGE THEM IN THINKING

Some bosses get irritated if people go to them too often. This is a chance to celebrate. Celebrate the fact that they trust you and your insights! It's more challenging to engage their thinking when you need to approach them (we'll explore that next) because they need to engage and haven't. When they come to you with an issue, it's already an active need in their mind, and the best time for them to learn is when their mind is actively exploring a topic. To solve the problem most efficiently, you need to get them to the main issue quickly.

Here are some ways you can choose to respond when your people come to you.

Ask "What Is Your Request?"

This is especially appropriate when they come to you with a complaint. Our brains can see wrong things ten times more than the right things. Without engaging our thinking skills, or without intent, we can easily look around and find a lot to complain about. One way to turn this around on your people is to ask the simple question, "What is your request?" This automatically engages their brain toward what they want to see happen (possibility-based thinking) versus what isn't happening or going well. Complaints can slip into never-ending spirals of negativity whereas requests are a step toward spiraling up toward improvement. This step can also help you, the coach, get to the heart of the matter and what's really on their mind.

Invite Them to Think with You

When your people come to you, make it easy for them to get right to the point and invite their thoughts by using the sentence "What's on your mind?" That is how you create the structure for a great coaching conversation. This question is beautiful for a few reasons.

First, it doesn't carry judgment. I once had a boss who'd ask what was wrong when I approached her. After a few months of this, I started to feel my energy draining every time I needed to interact with her. She approached our conversations with a default attitude that something was wrong (deficit-based thinking). I found myself avoiding her. Using *What's on your mind?* opens up the brain to possibilities and honors the potential of a problem or issue.

Second, this question implies that the recipient is already thinking. When you ask me what's on my mind, I go into my brain to see what I'm thinking. Other less-effective responses include *What's wrong?* or *What's up?* or *What's going on?* All three of these will elicit a response of the replay of a situation or a he said/she said recap of events and facts. And although those may certainly be helpful, starting with *thinking* often gets the conversation off on the right foot.

And third, it's been my experience that the question "What's on your mind?" cuts through chitchat and saves me, the coach, valuable time in my day.

Celebrate Their Ideas

This is the holy grail for bosses. When a team member comes to you with an idea, celebration is in order! This means they're thinking! However, I've seen some bosses shy away from encouraging thinking or idea generation because they aren't looking for ideas—they're only looking for good ideas.

We need to sort through a few ideas to get to the best ideas, so we could say that every idea is leading us to a good idea! Could we also say that there are no bad ideas? What if all ideas were celebrated? When someone comes to you with an idea, try the following phrases to help them continue thinking and exploring the idea with you:

- *Tell me more.* This encourages them with positive energy.

- *What problem are we solving here?* This ensures that their idea is relevant and focused on improvement.

- *What opportunities could we take advantage of?* This often gets them thinking in a bigger way.

- *How could this help?* This is a way to get the idea focused on results.

- *Who else have you run this by?* This encourages collaboration and transparency, helping them understand at a deep level that you're not the only person with whom they can collaborate.

Turn Requests for Information into Thinking Opportunities

Most often, employees need information. These requests probably take up most of your interaction time as a boss. These may include very simple questions such as

- Who is the contact at ABC supplier?

- What's the login for XYZ software?

- Have you seen the way the document is printing?

- Where did we decide to keep the new tools?

When faced with these requests, most bosses stop what they're doing and give a simple answer. If you want to engage thinking, you could reply with, "Where have you looked?" or "What have you tried?" or "Who else have you asked?" or my favorite, "Have you watched the video on that?" ☺ This approach to requests for information helps your people stop and think about resources to use other than the easiest one: you!

We experience this as parents too! "Mom! Where are my shoes?" Mom should say, "Where have you looked?" If my son has only looked in one spot before taking the easy way out and asking me, he usually doesn't even answer my question.

He heads out to look in more places. I foil his attempt for the easy way out with my questioning.

Basically, answer their question with your question. Over time, these question responses will save you time! Your people will become more self-reliant for the easy stuff, and they'll start coming to you as a thinking partner rather than an information terminal.

Enroll Them in the Solution to Their Issue

There are times when employees come to you with issues that only you can solve. I've seen lots of bosses state, "I'll take care of it." If you'd like to engage their thinking, enroll them in the solution with phrases like these:

- What would you do to solve the issue?

- What would your first step be?

- What would our first step be?

- What's the ideal outcome?

- What is your request?

- Help me think through this.

- I'd like your thoughts on how we could solve this together.

- What part of this solution can you be in charge of?

Note: Although your time management is outside the scope of this book, if you find yourself with a line of people outside your door needing your time and attention, applying the above techniques can help you shorten the length of that line. Also, keep in mind what we established in the Teach step, that it's difficult to do effective coaching if you haven't invested in the Teach step of the Thinking Advantage.

Another tool to consider is using group issue-solving sessions where your people can learn to count on peer-to-peer solutions rather than seeing you as the sole source. The Entrepreneurial Operating System has a meeting agenda and an Issues Solving Track that are effective for this.

The second way to engage in this coaching conversation step is when you initiate the conversation.

When You Go to Them

What happens when someone doesn't come to you for coaching when it could be helpful? First, let's examine what's going on in this person's brain. Just as some people come to you as the path of least resistance, *not* coming to you may be the path of least resistance for other people. For this type of person, coming to you could be painful for their ego or pride (the brain prioritizes ego protection over productivity). The little brother of being too proud to go to the boss is simply hesitancy, and when we dig into it, shame that they can't solve the problem themselves. That paralyzes people. They want to figure it out but are struggling. Ideally, through building trust and by living in an open and honest culture, your people will come to rely on you as a trusted coach.

Before we dive into how to go to them, let's address a few barriers to the *go to them method* that may be on your mind:

- *This takes so much time!* In practice, more time is spent worrying about the conversation than on the conversation itself. I've also witnessed bosses spending more time documenting infractions than it would have taken to simply have a conversation. Other bosses like to gather all the data points they'll need before having a conversation. How much time could you save yourself if you had the conversation without all the extreme preparation or sleepless worry?

- *I'll give the person or the situation the benefit of the doubt. It'll work itself out.* This happens when bosses don't address issues right away. As time goes by, the issue becomes less and less important in the short term, and we find ourselves assuming it won't happen again. We are disappointed when it does.

- *I don't want to be a micromanager; I give my people a task and get out of their way.* "Micromanager" is a term used to describe a boss who over-directs her team, someone who is sure there is only one way to reach a result. However, I've noticed that employees use the term even when humble interest or coaching is offered. There is a big difference. Don't miss out on a growth opportunity for you or your team by being fearful of micromanaging. Coaching isn't *managing* at all.

Here is a great way to overcome these barriers when going to your employees to initiate a coaching conversation: *Decide how you'll open by memorizing your first sentence.*

When I was a teenager, I had two after-school jobs. I'd drive about a mile from the school to our family business for my shift as a childcare worker where I wrangled, played with, and nurtured eight two-year-olds. When my shift was over, I sped about three miles south to either rehearse or perform at a small theatre for whatever production I was in at the time.

In each job, I learned the power of a memorized line. In working with two-year-olds, when it was time to clean up the toys, I had a catchy phrase (with an accompanying catchy tune) that I'd sing to indicate it was time to clean up. I didn't need to explain why we were cleaning up—the memorized line did it for me. In my roles at the theatre, I used memorized lines differently. I noticed that if I could remind myself of the first line of the scene, the rest of the scene came easily (after rehearsal, of course!). Even when I was in a long-running play, before I'd go on for a scene, I'd remind myself of my first line.

You can also use this concept to help you have the confidence to open up a coaching conversation. When used often, your people will know that a coaching conversation has begun. It's a cue to them that this is important, and their full presence of mind is requested.

A few years ago, I hired a marketing company to manage my website, direct me in social media, and put together media kits for potential speaking engagements. After a few months of working with the account manager they assigned me, I experienced poor results. During that time, I made the excuse that "It takes a while to get to know my voice; they'll get it soon," and, "They know way more about marketing than I do. I'll give them the benefit of the doubt that we'll soon get results. I'll just wait and see."

However, too many issues were piling up, and although I'd make comments about the issues here and there, I knew I needed to have a direct conversation. In worrying and preparing for this conversation, I decided that my opening line would be, "Tasha, this will be a difficult conversation." I chose that sentence because it wouldn't let me wimp out on not having the conversation. I also chose that line because Tasha and I are both glass-half-full people, and I needed to let her know, very clearly, that the water was muddy!

You may choose to have a handful of lines available to use in different situations. Here are some of my favorites:

- We had a miss here.

- I'd like your thoughts about _____. Do you have a minute to think it through with me?

- I'm concerned about _____. Can you help me understand the issues?

- I feel disconnected. Can we get on the same page about _____?

- I'm sensing/feeling (excited, nervous, anxious). Are you feeling that too? (This comes from you *observing* your feelings in Step One!)

- And a favorite from Kim Scott, author of *Radical Candor*, "I'm going to tell you something because if I were in your shoes, I'd want to know so I could fix it."

- Call me.

HELPING EMPLOYEES CHOOSE THEIR RESPONSE

In the Respond Mode of coaching, you are first choosing *your* response. Now, it's time to help those you're coaching choose *their* responses. We do this by getting them to think about their own thinking and getting them to identify clearly what we're trying to solve before we create the solution together. I've observed that the longer I spend in this phase (getting others to think clearly about choosing their response to the stimulus), the better the eventual solution sticks. I can't skip this part for time or get distracted. If I do and jump to co-creation, the issue eventually comes up again. Spend more time here, and the outcome will have a better chance of being favorable over the long term.

As you focus on adding your energy to helping your people become their best, remind yourself that in this mode you truly don't know or want to have the answer yet. You want the answer to come from the person you're coaching. This is where you, the coach, prove you have a possibility-based approach. You're confident that the *magic* is in them, not you.

This is probably a big shift for you. You've gained this leadership position because of the things you know and the answers you have. Now, I'm asking you to put that aside for a bit and really get curious by asking vs. telling.

Here are three ways to help you spend more time helping others think about their thinking:

Ask the Question behind the Question

The first stated question or issue is rarely the issue. (Our ego protects us from dealing with the real issue.) Getting to the root takes time (but sometimes only 30 seconds) and a question! Our brains can't ignore questions. When I'm coaching a client, the initial issue they ask for coaching on is rarely the real or core issue. Keep asking questions until you think they've really spent time thinking about the root issue.

Do They Need Direction or Support?

It's key that you know how they're arriving to the conversation. Do they need your direction because they really are out of ideas? Or do they need your support, meaning that they need you to listen and add your two cents or give a thumbs up for confidence? Both of these options involve getting the gears turning, but your approach in asking questions may be different.

Try starting with the question "What are your first thoughts?" to help you determine if they need direction or support. If they need your support or need you to poke holes in their plan/idea, they'll most likely start talking about the plan. If they need direction, you'll get a little less interaction at first.

Caution: When an employee just needs support and you give them direction, it offends their ego, in the psychological sense. They'll get emotionally defensive or offended, even if it's subtle. This puts friction between you and them rather than fostering connection. Keeping this simple, you can also try asking, "Do you need some direction or support in this?"

Active Silence

While getting them to think about their thinking and to choose their response, plenty of silence on your part is often a welcome gift. We live in a busy world with so much noise. Providing the space for them to think in silence is an oasis for the brain; positive effects can be observed in as little as two minutes.

You can use this in a casual way by reminding yourself to talk less; they should be doing most of the talking. An acronym that I keep close by on a sticky note as I coach is WAIT. It stands for "Why Am I Talking?" If you need to take a more organized approach to silence, say, "How about you and I both take two quiet minutes to think about [insert topic or question here] and write down our thoughts, then we'll share?" The third option is to ask the question and shut up. Humans are uncomfortable with silence. Be comfortable with silence and the real issue will often quickly be vocalized.

JUST ASK THE QUESTION
AND SHUT UP

Have a Lamppost Mindset

Even if you were as inanimate as a lamppost, it would be beneficial for your people to have this experience. Don't worry too much about asking the *right* questions or being perfect with this. You aren't the important one in this conversation. This is about them. Your only job is to be present with them as they think and talk.

Here's a final word about being in Respond Mode: When effective, Observe Mode and Respond Mode have a slow, effortless, curious feel to them. The pace is thoughtful, full of gaps of silence, exploration of different questions, and deep listening. In our busy achievement- and speed-oriented world, easing into these modes can feel counterproductive. That's when you know you're doing it right!

As a coach, I've experienced when leaders spend more time in Respond Mode, the next mode, Co-create, is faster. They find the right solution because they took the time to think clearly about the issue in the right way. You almost tell yourself that you don't want to know the answer; you only need to ask the right questions and be a good listening partner.

REFLECTION SECTION

1. Think of someone you know who regularly takes the coach approach and chooses their response. What responses do they choose?

   _____

   _____

2. What is your natural response (or reaction) to a negative event? What could you do to upgrade your existing response, even if just by one percent?

   _____

   _____

3. Where would you like to use your unlimited season pass of do-overs first? What is your first step in that action?

   _____

   _____

4. What is your memorized line?

   _____

   _____

5. In what situations could you use silence more effectively?

   _____

   _____

CO-CREATE MODE

FOUR MODES OF COACHING MAGIC

1. OBSERVE
2. RESPOND
3. CO-CREATE
4. RETURN & REFLECT

Co-creating happens when we come up with a solution together. It's not one-sided from either party. Using the Mastermind Effect, we collaborate, learning that two heads are always better than one. When we co-create solutions, we pull from the knowledge of both people. Co-creating can be done in a group as well.

When my son Brandon was 17, he spent his life's savings on a used Ford Mustang, which he cherished. I said one thousand times, "Drive slowly. Don't wreck. Stay off your cell phone, don't text and drive, and turn down your music!" Two weeks into ownership of this dream car, he totaled it. Sadness, anger, grief, and even depression followed.

This happens all the time in life! Though we've been told what to do, what to expect, and what the consequences of an action could be, somehow, we inevitably find ourselves in situations we didn't intend. We end up with regret and, often, someone has the opportunity to tell us, "I told you so!"

What's happening? Why is it that many of us need to learn things the hard way? Let's dissect Brandon's experience as it applies to what we've already explored in *The*

Thinking Advantage:

- Brandon experienced the *teaching* during his drivers ed courses.

- When I started *coaching* (behind-the-wheel time):

  ○ I *observed* that he wasn't taking the safety part of driving seriously. I observed that he acted as if he were invincible.

  ○ I chose the response of freaking out. I didn't even ask him to think about his response. I *reacted* with my instincts to protect my child. There was no inquiry, no space for thinking, and just lots of hinting, telling, and reminding! I did all the talking. Did he do any listening? Maybe his ears heard the sound of my voice, but the understanding that I thought I was communicating didn't click.

  ○ I didn't *co-create* with him. I took on the role of dictator. I mandated, threatened, and tried to instill fear by reminding him of consequences.

  ○ Once I knew he was physically okay, I told him to call the insurance company. They *rescued* him by sending him a check for the car.

  ○ Because he was so angry about the incident, I took the approach of letting him have his space, working it out on his own. I offered lots of compassion and told myself he'd learned his lesson. Fear of bringing up a painful experience had me avoiding the topic and getting his mind on something else. I didn't have the courage to invite him to *return and reflect*. We simply moved on.

Why is it so hard to learn from being told what to do? Because being told what to do causes us to skip the thinking. Doing what we're told takes very little effort. We're simply reacting. This pattern started in childhood, when most of the talking came from one direction: the adults. We started learning when we mimicked the adults' sounds and movements as infants. Later, as children, we followed their directions. (Or some of us did!) As we grew into teenagers, we had our ideas of how the world should be and often dabbled in the skill of debate with adults in authority. It was in this stage that we tried on new opinions, used bigger words, and became influenceable. We rarely had the experience of taking new-found knowledge and applying it in a rational way.

Therefore, teenagers and young adults often need to learn the hard way by having reality smack them in the face! Some of us learn lessons the hard way and then realize, *If I do what I'm told, then, next time, it won't be painful.* On the surface, this is beautiful and desirable. Yet, as we grow into adults and hold onto the mindset of just following the rules, we don't create the space for thinking.

WHEN PEOPLE WEIGH IN, THEY BUY IN

What we know about productivity and commitment also has a deeper effect when we apply it here using the Thinking Advantage. The management principle that "people must weigh in before they buy in" means that if you want someone to commit to a goal or solution, ask them what they think. Co-create Mode is all about getting people's ideas and opinions and helping them feel heard. When they feel heard, reasonable people can usually get behind the chosen idea, even if it's not theirs.

Caution: If we don't ask others to speak about what's on their mind, they'll do it anyway in less productive environments. People do this by internally ruminating on what they would've done, which leads to a lack of commitment to the ultimate decision. The other way is by talking to peers about an issue around the water cooler in a gossipy, secretive way. The third way they'll make sure they're heard is when the project has obstacles or fails. They'll make an I-never-thought-that-would-work-anyway type of comment. The act of co-creation prevents additional issues and adds fuel for making sure everyone is committed to the eventual outcome.

MY WAKEUP CALL

Every so often, I have a coaching experience that profoundly changes me. One particular day, I was in an Accountability Activator session with highly motivated service managers from around the country. These managers regularly dealt with issues involving auto parts, scheduling, dispatch, etc. These are things I know nothing about.

One of the activities in the workshop is what I call the clarity chair. This is where someone from the group—sometimes someone who is stuck on something—volunteers to come up to the stage and sit in the clarity chair to be coached by me in front of the group. I do this for a few reasons, one of which is I like the group managers to see what coaching looks like in real life. During the early hours of the workshop, the managers are learning the modes, learning why they work, and role-playing using their new skills. It's beneficial for everyone to see the parts all working together.

One quiet manager, Eduardo, volunteered to be coached. As I started using the modes with Eduardo, something happened that until that time, I'd never experienced: The coaching wasn't working. Ed wasn't responding the way he should have been. He was giving one-word answers, not digging deeper or past his original solution, not considering new ways of responding.

I began to get frustrated, and I remember thinking, *Why is Eduardo doing this to me? Doesn't he know what I'm trying to do here? Doesn't he want his colleagues to see great coaching? Why isn't he cooperating? He might be trying to sabotage this on purpose!* (Oh, how the brain likes to spiral up emotions when the ego is at risk.) I stopped the coaching session. I looked at the audience and said, "I'm stuck; this isn't working!" and that's when Ed said, "It's working for me ..."

What I failed to remember that day with Ed is that coaching is never about the coach. It's always about the person being coached. I let myself get too caught up in the spectacle of the performance. I focused on demonstrating the modes, showing my skills, and giving the audience a full circle example. No part of my coaching energy was focused on Ed. I still wonder if the session would've been more successful had I been observing at a deeper level. But I'm not sure I would choose a "do-over" since I experienced what happened next.

I hope you're not worried about Ed, because what happened after that had a big impact. As the managers in the group saw me give up, they took over. They started asking Ed questions, and he continued to respond. They moved effortlessly through the modes, finally co-creating some actions with him, never dictating. They were demonstrating the skills they'd learned that day. I faded into the background as I watched the entire group gain confidence in themselves and the modes. As a side note, as we were wrapping up, one manager said, "That was really cool how you pretended not to know what to do next and waited for us to jump in. I almost thought you were really stuck!"

It's always about the person you're coaching, not about you. When the coaching becomes about you, as it did with me that day, your default approach is to dictate. You tell people what to do, give them the answers, and give them directions rather than co-creating with them. I get this comment often from bosses: "But it's so much faster just to answer their questions!" Yes, it absolutely is. Today. But what about tomorrow and the next day? Using short-term thinking to quickly answer their questions without engaging their brains is always the easy way out for you. Although this may seem like what a boss *should* do on the surface, it kills any progress you've made in using the Thinking Advantage within your company. If you've been acting as a dictator, there's good news: You can start on the path to co-creation with a few easy skills.

CO-CREATE, DON'T DICTATE

Here are some ways to engage in co-creating instead of dictating:

Let Them Go First

When you move into Co-create Mode, ask the person you are coaching to share their ideas first. There are two big reasons why this is an approach that helps the thinking engage.

1. When you ask them to go first, you get to observe how they're thinking about the issue without your input. You'll be able to see if they're on or off track with their thinking, and you'll have a chance to get them back on track.

2. If you go first, they're less likely to think on their own. They'll rely on your thinking to get them to their answer. I like the phrases "What do you recommend?" and "What are your first thoughts on this?" or "What's your plan?" or "What's your next step on this?"

Build on Their Ideas

Let go of needing to have the perfect answer. The best answers are co-created. This is an approach that you probably use all the time. You're talking to someone with an idea, and you add your thoughts and twists, then they take your thought and enhance it or simplify it a bit, and together, you come up with something better than you could have on your own. You didn't have the answer, but with you, they found the answer. Or, in truth, you found it together! When you're building together, you use phrases with keywords like, "Oh!" or "And here's a twist we could consider ..." or "And what if we ..."

Offer Instead of Advise

I use this one frequently when someone has no idea where to start. This approach is helpful when someone says they need guidance vs. support. Instead of jumping in to tell them what to do, I like to offer a couple of things that they could try. I literally use the phrase "Here are a couple of things you could try." There are three main elements to this approach:

1. *Always offer more than one option.* I prefer three or more. When you offer multiple options or ideas, the person you're coaching will need to evaluate all of them, engaging in thinking.

2. *Always use the word "could," as in "Here are three things you could try."* Using *could* implies that they don't *need* to use any of them. Using this word also encourages the person you're coaching to feel free to use your idea or one of theirs and that the options are still malleable. I often witness clients using the options I've offered as a starting point or as material to work with to add to their idea. Using the word *should* instead of *could* removes this malleability, shuts down the thinking, and introduces the childhood dichotomy of obeying or rebelling into the conversation.

3. *Speak from experience*. Relate the three options to times when you've seen those options work. You may need to share a story of when you came across this same situation, a principle you found useful, a time you didn't take one of the options, and a time you failed. Being humble and real with this approach to co-creating is very powerful.

"You're right!"

Oftentimes, when you're co-creating with a direct report or a peer who is junior to you, you'll hear them say, "You're right, that's exactly what I should do." At first glance, this feels to you like a breakthrough, like clarity, like we're getting somewhere with this solution. And we are, but there's a lot of power packed into that sentence they used. When people say "you're right," they're giving you the power and credit for solving the issue. To create great thinkers, I like to use this dialogue:

Salina: "You're right, Jill. I should be having more great conversations with my people."

Jill: "Actually, Salina, *you're* right! If what I said feels right to you, then you're the one that's right. I simply offered you some options. But it sounds like you're sure of what your next step is. Did I hear that correctly?"

Using this technique when coaching increases Salina's confidence in her thinking and also reinforces the idea that the outcome is her choice. Additionally, if we let our direct reports say "you're right," then, if they fail, they also start to attribute their failure to your bad idea.

Leave the Coaching Experience with Clarity on the Action

As we learned when we examined the adult learning cycle, adults learn when we put things into action and when we're able to have an experience or interact with the thing we're learning. If we look at this step as purely engaging the brain in deep thinking and learning that sticks, this is a key ingredient in getting the brain mature. Adding in a large dose of reality and going back to this book's purpose, we want to create a thinking organization not for the sheer love of it, but because we want it to produce results!

This step becomes a no-brainer in the workplace. We need to decide and take action so that individuals, departments, and the company continue to get unstuck and move forward. Additionally, this is purely a major ingredient in good management. When we're coaching someone who isn't in the business (or even a peer in the business whom we don't manage), we might forget this step, ignore it, or feel that it's not our place to engage in this step. What helps me in times like this is to remember, as with my experience with Eduardo, that coaching isn't about me; it's always about the person I'm coaching. If I'm really invested in helping them become their best, I'll invite them to decide on their next step, even if I'm not their direct manager. Here are some ways to help them decide on their next step.

What feels right to you?

Similar to the *you're right* approach, this one involves proactively asking the person you're coaching to think about how they're feeling about the next step. When you ask the question this way, it's the opposite of saying, "So, here's what you should do." Another variation of this is when they're asking for your opinion on the next steps and there are two good options, you could say, "I've seen it work both ways; what feels right to you?"

What will you do next?

More often than not, what really needs to be co-created and decided upon is simply the next step, not the entire solution or entire plan. Life, business, projects, and people are iterative anyway. So many variables are involved, and we live in a complex world. When we ask, "What are you going to do next?" we're asking for the next step, not a solution that will solve everything. "What will you do next?" is a simplifying sentence for the brain.

GETTING PEOPLE TO VERBALIZE THE OBSTACLES GETS THEM OUT OF THEIR HEAD AND INTO SOLUTION MODE.

What might get in your way?

By asking people to verbalize the obstacles, you're setting them up for success. The brain is great at identifying obstacles, but we don't naturally want to talk about them. However, when we do talk about them, we see more possibilities for overcoming them. We'll be able to prevent them and co-create solutions that will lead to solid outcomes. Otherwise, we tend to ruminate.

Ruminating is thinking about the same thing repeatedly with no clarity on the next steps, no learning, and no extraction of value. If we ruminate on the obstacles, it's harder to find solutions, and we just add fuel to our worries. Worry is a poor use of the creative brain and takes up so much energy. Getting people to verbalize the obstacles gets them out of their head and ready to come up with solutions.

What will you try first?

This question works well when someone says, "I don't know." It helps them ease into an attitude of experimentation rather than perfectionism. Rarely are we exactly positive that our efforts will bring about the desired outcome. But we choose a response or decide on an action that will get us closest to that desired outcome. We don't need to *know* that this action will work, but in asking the question, "What will you try first?" we're asking them to engage in probability thinking.

What is your best guess?

This also implies that there needs to be some action taken, even if it's wrong. To paraphrase Theodore Roosevelt, the best thing we can do right now is to make the right decision. The second-best thing we can do is to make the wrong decision. The worst thing we can do is to make no decision or take no action.

Here's what I would do and why.

Use this one sparingly, most often only after they've come up with some ideas and engaged in thinking with you. I use this when I know that they need direction and are starting to form their thinking skills. If you use this too early in the conversation, it's just dictating, and you'll foster dependency on you for the thinking. You can share an experience, a new principle, a new mindset, or a story. Humans love to engage with stories, and they're very impactful for learning.

Recall the experience Brandon had totaling his car. Had I shared my experience of being in a car accident when I was 17, would he have been able to think about his driving at a deeper level? I shared my story with him after his accident to help him feel normal, but sharing the story as he learned to drive didn't occur to me. We can use stories of failure or our learning when coaching others. Sometimes, it's the main thing they'll remember from the interaction.

Finally, make sure your recommendation comes with a *why*. Tie it back to the bigger picture for them. Maybe the bigger picture is part of your company's one-year plan? Maybe the bigger picture is supporting the core values? Maybe the bigger picture is getting them focused on their highest priorities. Following this statement with a loop back to "What feels right to you?" will help them know that it's still their decision.

By when?

We are time-based creatures. We work so efficiently with time-based goals. Adding this two-word phrase to the end of your conversation kicks the brain into action. Without addressing this, all the co-creation that just happened remains a thought, not an action. The brain doesn't put anything on its priority list until there is a due date!

Possibility and Encouragement

I like to leave all conversations with a possibility focus and a word of encouragement. Most of the time, these encouragements come in one of three forms.

It's normal, and you're normal!

Leaders are known to feel isolated, like they're the only ones experiencing these issues or having these experiences. When I let them know that these issues are normal, it helps them take their actions with a more positive mindset.

Growth-minded grit!

I remind them that this experience is essential for their growth, and if they can do this, they'll be able to solve this issue better and faster next time. The obstacle *is* the way! Embrace it and celebrate it.

I'm on your team!

Sometimes, people just need to be reminded that they have a support system. If a leader is feeling particularly isolated, I remind them that I'm with them. One of the visionaries I coach told me the reason he appreciates my coaching is he knows I'm *for* him, as in, I'm in his court, on his team, and rooting for his success. Leaving the conversation knowing that someone is for you strengthens your confidence.

SIMPLICITY IN CO-CREATING SOLUTIONS

Let's go all the way back to the beginning of why coaching works. It works because our world is very complex, and coaching helps simplify that world. I've experienced that when I do very effective co-creating, it most often ends up looking like one of these four simple outcomes.

Having Conversations

About 90% of the time, the simple solution is to have a conversation with someone. A few years ago, at the end of a busy yet powerful day of coaching leaders from more than ten companies in ten different coaching sessions, my mind was exhausted, full, and busy. When my mind gets this way, I like to take a few minutes to put everything in perspective. It helps me slow things back down so I can ease into turning my mind off.

On this particular day, I had a big aha moment as I reflected on the day. One hundred percent of the solutions that I co-created with my clients resulted in them deciding to have conversations. One CEO decided that she needed to have a conversation with her integrator. One sales manager decided he needed to have a conversation with a client. And one membership team member decided to have a conversation with a potential partner. Every one of the sessions that day resulted in the need for some kind of conversation. This isn't always the case, but after that day, I was more aware when this was the outcome and wasn't surprised when this followed the Pareto principle: 80% of the time, having a conversation is the solution that gets clarity and is the simplest answer. That led me to using the phrase, "When in doubt, have a conversation." What kind of conversation? A coaching conversation!

Experimenting

Often, the outcome of effective co-creating is that the person I'm coaching decides to experiment with a solution. This involves trying something new: a new structure, new role, new metrics, new Meeting Pulse, new idea. One leader of several companies (with the same owner) had the idea that the companies could benefit from running as one entity. We co-created a solution: He was going to experiment with combined meetings to see if there was any benefit to solving issues together. His companies would try sharing a Scorecard, Rocks, and to-dos. Instead of assuming there was a benefit, he was going to experiment to see if it really did work better.

Changing the One Big Thing That Fixes Many Little Things

Often, after seeing the root cause of an issue, people tend to make big, systemic decisions. These cause big changes that affect many symptomatic issues for the better. Next, big leaps of inspiration and courage occur. Sometimes decisions like this come from not solving the issue at the root after several attempts. Sometimes these come from a single event that highlighted the root cause.

One afternoon, during a coaching call, the top leader of a $25-million construction company asked me a question: "Do I need to be at the Jill level of coaching to get this company to $65 million in revenue?" We'd just finished an annual session where we'd experienced a few key breakthroughs, and he attributed it to my coaching skills. He felt that until he could coach as I did, the company wouldn't reach its goals. I shared with him that although I had led the coaching, it was the team that made the decisions.

He was feeling ready for his next level, so I reflected to him what I'd observed during our annual session. I saw him make bigger decisions than he'd ever made before. Having a great coach certainly helps one have confidence in making big decisions, but it's the decisions and actions that build a company, not the coaching. Then I asked, "What big decisions are you not making?" He didn't even need to think about it; he knew what additional big decisions needed to be made. In the next six months, this company made legal changes to their operating structure, shut down a department, and made additional changes to the leadership team. These were big decisions that were holding the company back and automatically resolved many symptomatic issues.

Taking Time to Think

Occasionally, the outcome is that the person you're coaching gains clarity about what they need to think about. Next, they'll benefit from some time thinking on their own. For example, one leader I coached recently decided that he needed to hire an assistant to solve his issue of needing more time. His next step was to think about and write down what he'd like to delegate to that assistant before looking for that person. Had the action been to start looking before he really thought about what he wanted, he might have hired the wrong person. Sometimes, coaching focuses, re-focuses, and re-energizes someone to do more deep thinking on their own. Don't discount this as an effective next step.

REFLECTION SECTION

1. What are the differences between compromising and co-creating solutions? What elements are present when you observe co-creation? In comparison, what does compromise feel like?

    _____
    _____
    _____
    _____

2. In what areas of your life are you a dictator? Name instances when you would rather tell people what to do than co-create. How could you dictate even one percent less in these areas?

    _____
    _____
    _____
    _____

3. Are there people who rely on you for co-creation? Are there people who rely on you to be a dictator? How could you enroll these people in better or more co-creation?

    _____
    _____
    _____
    _____

4. On whom do _you_ rely for co-creation? What do you appreciate about their approach?

    _____
    _____
    _____
    _____

With all of this momentum in the Co-create Mode, it's easy for a novice coach to think that their job is done. You've observed, chosen your response, helped the person think about their thinking, and co-created a solution together! The person you've coached is off and running, unstuck, feeling productive, and moving toward the goal once again.

But coaching people has one more step, and it's a step that we rarely engage in, yet it has the most potential for ensuring that the learning sticks. This is when we add a simple phrase to the end of the coaching session such as, "Hey, Tonya, when you are done with that, come back and let me know how it went." This is when you enter the fourth mode of Coaching Magic.

RETURN AND REFLECT MODE

FOUR MODES OF COACHING MAGIC

1 OBSERVE
2 RESPOND
3 CO-CREATE
4 RETURN & REFLECT

Return and Reflect is so incredible that it shows up twice in this book! It is both the final mode of Coaching Magic and the final step in the Thinking Advantage. We'll explore this step in-depth in Step Four, but I'll touch on it here as it relates to coaching.

At first glance and at a meta-level, there are no major differences in this step in either of the algorithms. The main concept is to provide a space for the person you're coaching to reflect verbally on the experience they just had. You simply say, "Hey, Kim, when you've done [whatever solution it was that you co-created], let me know how it went." However, there is one shift in mindset here when you're approaching this from a purely coaching role rather than from a manager role. We know that coaching can be very effective in the role of a manager. But the coaching role can also be very powerful when used with peers, vendors, third parties, contractors, clients, and friends.

**COACHING CAN BE USED
VERY EFFECTIVELY
IN THE ROLE OF A MANAGER.**

**BUT THE COACHING ROLE
CAN ALSO BE VERY POWERFUL
WHEN USED WITH**
- **PEERS**
- **VENDORS**
- **THIRD PARTIES**
- **CONTRACTORS**
- **CLIENTS AND FRIENDS**

Pure coaching is possible even if the coach has no expertise in the issue or problem. And that's part of the magic! The magic here in Return and Reflect Mode is that by offering the opportunity for the person you're coaching to reflect on their experience, they're doing all the work and learning as they talk. You simply ask the question and listen. It's almost as if you, the coach, aren't needed for this mode, except to receive the words they're saying. Psychologists call this being an *empathetic witness*, where the listener (or coach) simply listens without judgment and repeats or summarizes for clarity. In a more lighthearted way, Michael Neill, the author of many books on coaching, refers to this as the *lamppost effect*. If the coach could be as inanimate as a lamppost, the client would still benefit from the session.

If coaching is the number one skill for the 21st century, how can you dedicate yourself to mastering this skill with your direct reports and anyone else that you care to add energy to? What kind of company would you run if you used coaching to help people become their best?

Now more than ever (as I finish this book in the middle of a global health crisis), people are hungry for coaching. They need to get unstuck. They crave certainty in their next steps and need simplicity to engage their thinking skills. What if you could be the thinking partner they need?

REFLECTION SECTION

FOUR MODES OF
COACHING MAGIC

1 OBSERVE

2 RESPOND

3 CO-CREATE

4 RETURN & REFLECT

1. Of the four coaching modes, which one will be the hardest for you to try? Why?

    _____

    _____

2. Which mode or modes are you the most confident about?

    _____

    _____

3. Besides your boss, name some people who coach you.

    _____

    _____

4. In which ways would you like your boss to coach you more effectively?

    _____

    _____

5. Who on your team could benefit from being coached?

    _____

    _____

STEP THREE
DON'T RESCUE

 TEACH

 COACH

 DON'T RESCUE

 RETURN & REFLECT

We love heroic tales, don't we? We love to hear stories of heroes and have a high regard for them. This is something that spans all cultures. Joseph Campbell, author of *The Hero with a Thousand Faces*, did comprehensive research on mythological narratives from ancient and modern literature across the world's cultures and concluded that all good stories follow a "hero's journey" pattern. It's what makes for a great story.

The unlikely hero is faced with a challenge that he or she doesn't seek but feels compelled to complete. They have a few challenges/disasters, learn from those challenges, experience great change, fight the "enemy" and win, and then return home to a normal, yet somehow changed, life.

If the stories we've been living with elicit so much reverence for the hero, it's no wonder we engage in and get excited about being heroic. I love being heroic! It's even part of my daily affirmations. In fact, it's number one! "I am a hero! I have strength for two and create other heroes in my wake."

Remember the two friends jumping in the river to save the drowning kids? They were heroes! They saved people from drowning! However, as with all good things, there can be too much of it. And that's what this next step is all about. Going overboard with your heroism prevents the opportunity for your people to do some of their thinking.

A MORE THOUGHTFUL HERO

If we really want to teach people how to think, they must be able to have an experience. This is the exact same reason why we let them practice and use the training right away when we're teaching. Experiencing tough situations, working hard to get a result, and facing new or difficult tasks is novel to the brain and causes the brain to pay closer attention. When we do the same things repeatedly and are exposed to a limited number of new experiences, we become stagnant, and our brain goes into coasting mode. Having experiences is all about being encouraged, experimenting, and increasing your people's thinking ability.

DON'T TAKE THE MONKEY!

I first came across the concept of the monkey when reading *The One Minute Manager Meets the Monkey* by Ken Blanchard. (Ken gave credit to William Oncken Jr. for the concept.) I highly recommend that you read this short yet powerful book, but here is the concept in a nutshell. Most managers want to be helpful (a hero) to their people. It's human nature to want to help. When another human asks you, "Can you help me out?" it's painful for you to say no. Since managers are also human, they get in a trap of helping their people too often. In this book, we'll call it *rescuing* because the manager has a mindset that the employee needs them or they'll drown!

What ends up happening (spoiler alert for Blanchard's book) is the manager becomes the dumping ground for all the hard, uncomfortable, or unpleasant tasks. They pile up on the manager's desk or to-do list and go undone, causing the manager to either work longer days or have more stress. Blanchard and Oncken call these tasks monkeys because they multiply, cause chaos, and it's hard to shake them. When I'm teaching Accountability Activator workshops, I often hand out toy monkeys for the bosses to take home to remind them not to rescue people by taking their monkeys.

Here is an illustration of non-recommended monkey-taking in action! Sam has come to you for coaching. He's concerned because a client is upset, and he's afraid the client will leave. After co-creating the action together (he decided that offering the client a revision to the contract and requesting increased cooperation from the client's team would be the best solution), Sam's next step is to make a phone call to the client to propose the solution. But you, the boss, start to get nervous. Sam has never made a big phone call like this. You have—you've had dozens of calls like this, and you've learned the fine art of finesse, listening, empathizing, and negotiation. You could say these are your best skills! And this is a big client. During your coaching, you offered Sam a few different ideas, and you're pretty sure they soaked in, but you're still hesitant for some reason.

Let's pause the story right here to examine what's going on in your brain. The brain is a complex organ, but here are some highlights you should be aware of in these situations.

1. Your Fear Center (Amygdala)

This is the part of your brain that protects you from pain and suffering. This part of the brain will encourage you to choose the most successful solution with the least risk to your physical well-being. Even if it's subconsciously, the story you tell yourself is, *If Sam messes this up, the client will leave. I'll get fired. I won't get another job. I'll lose my paycheck, my house, and my kids will go hungry, and I'll end up living in a van down by the river!*

Even when you intellectually know that's not true, your brain, if left unrestrained, will plant these thoughts in your head to protect you from physical harm. Gratefully, our prefrontal cortex (the logic center) has evolved to partner with our amygdala, and we can consciously acknowledge the protective thoughts, then act rationally.

2. Your Efficiency Center

We're efficient creatures and naturally prioritize the present over the future. This part of your brain will encourage you to take the shortest route to success. Because we've evolved to conserve energy, our brains tell us stories that sound like this: *It's easier for me just to do it myself. I know the client really well, and this will sound better coming from me. I don't want to distract Sam preparing for this difficult conversation; he has other things to do. I don't need to prepare at all, so this will be faster for everyone. I need to call the client anyway about this other thing, so it'll save us both time. I'll see the client next week at the trade show anyway, so I'll talk to them then.* Oh, the way we tell ourselves stories!

3. Your Ego Center

And this may be the trickiest to acknowledge. Forgive me if you feel you need some life coaching after this section, but here's the truth: You may love to rescue your people because it feels good to you. It feeds your ego to know your people need you to save them.

Your brain may also be telling you stories like, *The helpful thing to do would be to put Sam out of his pain. It would be so nice of you to do this for him. It will really relieve him of having to be in a tough conversation. You are a good person to help him in this way; he'll be so grateful and probably remember this moment for the rest of his life! You're really valuable here. No one can do this as well as you can. It's a good idea for the person who is best at the task in the company to do the task. This is exactly what a good boss does for their people. This is what a great company looks like, helping each other out. We've built a great culture of teamwork!* And finally, *This is job security! Having me around to do these hard tasks means that I'm valuable.*

Knowing about and acknowledging these three points is often all it takes to start rescuing your people less, but since this book is all about getting everyone to use the Thinking Advantage, it's also powerful to recognize what's going on in the mind of your employee, Sam. So, let's examine what's going on in his brain right now.

Remember, the scenario is you've co-created an action, and he's about to leave your office to go talk to the client.

Say you choose to rescue him by saying something like, "Sam, I'm going to see the client on Thursday at an industry event anyway. Let me talk with her; I know her really well, and maybe this will go over better when it's coming from me. She'll know we're taking it seriously." Let's look at what would be going on in Sam's brain in this rescuing scenario:

1. His Efficiency Center

His efficiency center is taking note of this rescue. Brains love to create patterns and attach meaning to these patterns. Brains take note of what works and what doesn't work for efficiency. Right now, his brain is celebrating and remembering what worked. Essentially, it says to itself, *Yes! Getting my boss to help me with a solution is really efficient. I won't need to do any additional work because he is going to do the work for me. I'll remember this for next time!* The brain makes a connection that says, *Go to your boss the next time you're stuck, and you won't need to work as hard!* Keep in mind that these are rarely conscious thoughts; they are deep and subtle, yet very powerful.

2. His Pain Center

His pain center is in relief! He was, at his core, fearful of having this interaction with the client. You just took that pain away. When we have a sense of relief, the chemicals oxytocin and dopamine (and several others outside the scope of this book) flood our brains, and we connect the person involved in the interaction to the feeling. This rescue seals in Sam's brain that this other person (in this case, you—the boss) can help him feel happier and take pain away. He'll start to have feelings of admiration and love for this person. Sam may think, *I love working here! I love my boss. My boss is the best. I'm so lucky to have a boss that's so helpful. My boss is a good guy.* You may also hear Sam saying these words out loud, to you and others as well. "Thank you so much! That would be really helpful."

So, what's wrong with these above scenarios in Sam's brain? Everything seems so awesome! Well, it's the next part that kills the thinking part of his brain.

3. His Ego Center

Sam's ego center has been attacked. In this case, we're talking about the psychological ego: the sense of self, or self-confidence. To become great thinkers and really have the Thinking Advantage, we need to believe that we *can*. Although Sam is excited about being efficient and pain-free right now, his ego center is saying, *My boss doesn't believe in me. I'm not ready for this level of thinking yet. I'm still in training. I can't do hard things. I should stick to the easy thing. It's going to be a long time before I can handle something like this on my own. If the boss had to do it for me, it must require boss-level skills that I don't have.*

Then, Sam's brain seals all of this in by concluding, *The best way for me to move ahead is to depend on my boss. He knows what to do and will do the hard stuff that I can't do.* Next week, you'll find Sam in your office again because he's trained in being rescued.

Now, let's play this scenario again, this time observing what happens in your brain and Sam's brain when you do *not* rescue.

Remember: You've co-created the solution, and Sam is about to leave your office. You've offered him some guidance and asked enough questions for him to have had space to think about his approach, and although he's nervous, he's ready to make the call.

1. Your Fear Center

Without this great coaching you've provided for Sam, your pain center would be in a full panic, but since the two of you co-created the solution and agreed on the best approach, you're in less pain than you thought. You're still worried, and this causes you some stress. You don't know what's happening at each moment, but you can use the Return and Reflect step to help reduce this fear.

2. Your Efficiency Center

This one is elated! You didn't add any tasks to your list. You're allowed to work with full efficiency! (This is similar to the feeling you get after saying no.)

3. Your Ego Center

There's a lot going on here! Even if you're used to interacting with people this way, humans still tend to second guess themselves. You may hear yourself having thoughts like, *Why did I think Sam could do this on his own? He probably feels like I fed him to the wolves! I bet he's so mad at me right now. Is that really a way to support your team? If he fails, will it make me look bad? We can't afford for this to go wrong! What were you thinking, self?*

Now let's look at Sam's brain:

1. His Fear Center

He's feeling some healthy pressure right now, but it's supported by your good coaching. He's growing, and since there is a bit of fear, he's very focused.

2. His Efficiency Center

He's totally focused here too! He wants to succeed. He wants to gain a new capability that will make his life easier in the future. When we're learning, our brains pay close attention to what works and doesn't work. We release some adrenaline. This hyperfocus on doing well and learning something that will enhance our future is what happens when the part of our brain responsible for learning is lit up and ready for programming! Because you provided good coaching through conversation, you took advantage of the fact that talking enables the learning center.

3. His Ego Center

There are huge benefits to his ego. His ego is thinking, *My boss believes in me. He thinks I'm ready to take on critical tasks. This is important to the company, and I'm the one in charge. I must be really good at this. I can do hard things. I'm well-supported here. I'm critical to success here.*

As we've explored in the above scenarios, when we don't rescue our people, we enable them to have a learning experience. These experiences, especially when novel or new, create additional knowledge that really sticks and moves a person forward forever.

EXPERIENCES,
ESPECIALLY WHEN NOVEL OR NEW, CREATE ADDITIONAL KNOWLEDGE THAT REALLY STICKS.

WHEN YOU CAN SEE FARTHER DOWN THE RIVER

One of the fun games I like to play with my three boys is the game "How have I ruined your life forever?" Typing that sounds harsh, but this game gets us giggling and able to reflect on how we were thinking *then* and how we are thinking *now*. (Yes, it's a trick to get my teenagers to have deep conversations and talk about the growth mindset.)

One of the stories that comes up every year or so is about a time when I took Dillon and Tyler to Big Rock Park in Glen Rose, Texas. This is an out-of-the-way, hidden place that has dozens of big rocks the boys love to jump and climb on. There is also a shallow river that is the right balance between safety and adventure. A five-year-old can float down and then easily stand up and walk back up the river to do it again.

There is a dam and a short, six-foot angled spillway just before the safe, shallow part of the river. On this particular day, we walked up to the edge of the dam where the boys, who were two and five at the time, threw rocks and sticks. The edges of the dam were slanted concrete, so five-year-old Tyler could wade in a few inches or so and still feel comfortable. After a few minutes, he got a little too confident, miscalculated, and slipped into the dam's deep part and was swept down the river. I still remember the look of terror on his face as he looked up to me, needing a rescue.

As is often the case when parents are faced with danger, I quickly calculated the situation. Many details jumped to my mind all at once. Tyler, although only five, was a great swimmer. Dillon, a toddler, standing two feet to the side of me, was not. If I jumped in to save Tyler, would Dillon follow me and be in worse danger? Could I really pull both of them out of the river if that were the case? From my perch on the bank, I also estimated that Tyler was only about 20 feet away from the shallow spillway. I could see that as soon as he got to that point, he could let his body slide down the spillway to where he'd land in the 12 inches of water in the safer part of the river.

So, that's what I did. I chose not to jump in to save him, but instead, I hustled along the bank with Dillon and shouted instructions to Tyler, outlining my plan and what was ahead. The problem was that, from Tyler's point of view, he was swept down a river and his mother wasn't coming to rescue him. From his angle, he couldn't see that safety was only seconds away, and he felt deserted. The story is now known in our family as "The Day Mom Let Tyler Drown."

As bosses, we are often able to see farther ahead down-river than our people. We can calculate a little faster, see the risks and rewards a little clearer. Our people often have a different perspective and may feel deserted when we won't give them an answer right away or let them struggle with something before offering help. We know that they'll be okay and even better off because of the struggle.

Be aware that when you don't rescue your people, as I didn't rescue Tyler, they may at first resist, get discouraged, and feel pain. This is all part of the process. When you can see that the learning they're about to experience will benefit them more than the risk involved if they fail, it's time to let the learning begin. And let's remind ourselves that the learning that happens when you *don't* rescue is enabled because you have strong teaching and coaching in place.

Here are some strategies that you can try when you want to take charge of your brain and make rescuing a habit of the past!

1. Co-create

Being part of the solution helps you have confidence in its outcome and creates a space where an agreement can be made. This is in contrast to a direct order from you or the team going with the first idea presented.

2. Role-play

If you're nervous or they're nervous, spend some time role-playing using the 80% Approach™. The 80% Approach (developed by Dan Sullivan) states that the first time you do anything, the best it can ever be is 80% awesome. Do that same thing again, and you can get closer to 96%. Do that same thing a third time, and you can get as close to perfect as possible (99.2%). So, if you role-play three times, the major mistakes will usually happen during the first and second tries. This will give you and the person you're coaching more confidence to follow through with the co-created action.

3. Do the Action with Them

I've seen this approach work well, especially when people are teaching a technical skill. Think back to our previous scenario, when Sam was about to have a conversation with the client. This principle prescribes that both Sam and his boss would be on the call. Sam would do most of the talking, but the boss might interject a few thoughts.

This is my favorite way to learn a new skill. When my boys are teaching me to play a new game, I'll often ask if I can watch them do it first, then I want to try it myself with them very close by. Once I get the basics, I want them to go easy on me the first few rounds as my opponent, and I always appreciate their coaching as I increase my skills.

In summary, when your company is functioning with the Thinking Advantage, you'll have managers and coworkers who engage in less rescuing! Great managers learn to let their people fail a bit to learn from experience and know what to do differently next time. Great managers often assign surprisingly substantial projects to their direct reports to help them stretch and grow. They know that if the team member fails to get results from the growth task, all is not lost. In fact, much knowledge is gained because *actual* thinking was involved. Great managers know that success is a poor teacher, but a FAIL is just the "First Attempt In Learning." This is a powerful and true human learning and development concept. This is why we need a great plan not to rescue our people.

THE FIRE DEPARTMENT TOOL

And yet …

> Everybody has a plan until they
> get punched in the mouth.
> —Mike Tyson

Every manager wants to help their people learn and grow, until that learning and growing is causing a major disaster.

It's not reality to pretend we're never going to rescue again because we know the effects on the brain and learning. When I calculated from the riverbank and decided not to jump in to save Tyler, it was because I saw he was going to survive. Had I believed his life was at risk, I certainly would have rescued him. To think that we should never rescue is just a big slice of utopia pie. However, when you do need to rescue, the rescue can still be used as an opportunity for your people to engage in deep thinking.

Have you ever stopped to wonder or observe how a city fire department works? As the public, we see heroes who regularly save lives and show great courage in the face of real or possible danger. They literally rescue people. That's the part we see and hear about. You could even say it's the sexy part!

Great stories of heroism make the newspaper and social media, but what we don't see is that fire departments spend most of their time focusing on fire prevention. They regularly make unannounced visits to businesses to ensure they are up to fire code and offer fire prevention education to the community. They warn the community when risks are high and enforce the rules when someone isn't following them. They put lots of thought, organization, and effort into preventing fires, and yet, fires still happen.

When the fire is detected, the first thing the fire department does is, quite simply, *extinguish the fire!* They *rescue* the people and pets!

But when the fire is out and the people are rescued, their job isn't over. They go back to the fire once the embers have cooled, and they investigate. They dig to discover the cause of the fire, ask multiple questions of the witnesses or people involved, and report their findings.

Why do they do this? (We'll leave the insurance companies out of this example for now. ☺) They do this to continue to learn and educate ourselves on how to prevent a fire next time. What if we took that approach when we rescued our people or put out their proverbial fires?

Here's how you can be more like a fire department and help your people learn how to think, even when rescue is involved.

Step One: Put Out the Fire

Do it. Rescue your people. Do it for them—take the task right out of their hands if something is on fire. But step two and three must follow for this tool to work.

Step Two: Put That Issue on the Issues List

In EOS, an Issues List is a parking lot of obstacles, barriers, ideas, and opportunities. If you're running your company on EOS and you've rolled it out completely, every person in your company will have access to an issues list. If you don't have one, you can start one right away by taping a piece of paper to a wall and writing the word *issues* at the top. It's that simple! After you've put out the fire, put that fire on the list.

One of my clients installs flooring for large corporate buildings. One day, an installer started to spread the concrete and found that the color seemed off. When he asked his boss what to do, his boss had to tell him exactly what to do to remedy the situation. Otherwise, it would have been a million-dollar mistake.

In theory, the boss could have coached the employee by asking him to think through what the causes could be, asking him about his process, reviewing a training video, etc. But that approach would have been irresponsible toward the client and the company. The boss quickly made the changes necessary, and the job got back on track immediately!

Most managers leave the situation there, and everyone breathes a sigh of relief. The manager is the hero again, and all is well. But a great manager adds this issue to the list, and the issue isn't solved. The embers of that fire are still glowing and are about to flare up again at any moment.

Step Three: Solve the Issue Forever as a Team Using the IDS™ Pattern

Great managers have a set time, usually once a week, to work through issues. By saving the topic for this meeting, they ensure that they can follow the IDS pattern in a methodical way to get to the heart of the issues (the hot embers, if you will).

The Issues Solving Track in EOS teaches that to solve issues effectively, first, you need to *Identify* the issue at its root, then *Discuss* ideas related to solving that root issue, then *Solve* the issue by deciding what needs to be done next. By solving the issue as a team, everyone gets a chance to think out loud, ask what went wrong, discuss the scenario, think of possible solutions for next time, and have additional training if necessary. This is where you can solve for the long term and prevent fires too.

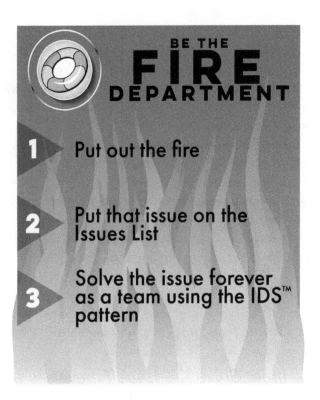

To create the Thinking Advantage, we've now learned how to engage our people in teaching, we've explored the four modes of Coaching Magic, and we didn't rescue, so now comes the last step in the algorithm. This one is the easiest and simplest, and it seals in the learning! When this step is completed, thinking is likely to become a habit, and it will become exponentially valuable to your company!

REFLECTION SECTION

1. Think of a time when you were rescued by a boss. Can you see any patterns of thought in how you felt when this happened?

   _____

   _____

2. How do you feel when you rescue people? Reflect for a moment on how much of your confidence is based on helping other people.

   _____

   _____

3. Write a few sentences about the difference between coaching people and rescuing people.

   _____

   _____

4. Think of a time when you rescued someone. Was it a true fire you were saving them from? If not, what would you do differently next time to create more thinking in your company?

   _____

   _____

5. Name someone on your team right now that you rescue more often than is necessary.

   _____

   _____

STEP FOUR

RETURN AND REFLECT

 TEACH

 COACH

 DON'T RESCUE

 RETURN& REFLECT

EXPERIENCE IS A HOT COMMODITY!

When we create a job ad, we often state things like "five years' experience required" or "ten years' experience a must." Why? Because it's a no-brainer that if people have "been there, done that" they will most likely come to work and be here and do that for us! They'll be more productive and make fewer mistakes if they have experience.

This final step in the Thinking Advantage is a multiplier of experience. Imagine this: you've just *coached* your team member through something they were stuck on, you *co-created* a solution, and you didn't *rescue* them. They, very literally, just had an experience. And we've already established that experience is valuable. Engaging in a moment of *reflection* can help that experience sink in, stick, and offer deeper context the next time a similar situation arises.

EXPERIENCE WITHOUT REFLECTION WILL BE FORGOTTEN.

And that's only because we're human! Let's head back to what we know about the brain to see why.

This person's experience, up until now, was raw material in their brain. They tried things that didn't work, found things that did work, found a new partner, had a hard conversation, struggled with painful moments, had some powerful aha moments, etc. All of this is great. They also had other experiences that were less meaningful, like having breakfast, answering the phone, being stuck at a stoplight, and mindlessly scrolling through social media.

The point is, a lot of information entered their brain that day. If we don't take time to seal in those meaningful experiences, the brain will wash them away and treat them as irrelevant. Here's how that works. As you sleep, your brain cells shrink microscopically, then your cerebral spinal fluid moves in and out of your brain cells, washing and cleaning them up for the next day. If you don't tag the meaningful experiences as valuable memories, they're at risk of disappearing with the trash. Why would we let that happen? We invested time and attention into coaching this person; don't waste the investment! Make it work for you again and again with this simple step.

By simply offering them time to reflect on their experience, the learning from that experience is more likely to stick.

USE RETURN AND REFLECT IN TWO EASY STEPS

1. Return: Make the Invitation!

Invite the person back with a simple phrase like, "When you're done, come on back and let me know how it went." The invitation alone sets their mind on a path of thinking *I'm going to report all of this,* and that gives the action more intention (and attention). Their brain automatically starts taking note of things to report, even if it's not totally conscious. As a bonus, they feel you care about and place importance on the situation, and it becomes a trust-building experience.

Whenever I teach this tool, bosses often report that they ask people to come back, but they rarely do. If you find yourself experiencing the same thing, here are a few things to remember:

Don't worry about it.

As a coach, I make it a point to end every coaching conversation with an invitation. Sometimes they accept my request, and sometimes they don't. When they do, they feel the power of reflection and walk away with more learning. The experience is elevated, and they can apply what they've learned to more than just one scenario. I love the Return and Reflect conversations because this is where the transformation really occurs as they can see their experience with a new perspective now that the experience is over. Some leaders take me up on my coaching and others don't, but I've come to a happy place by knowing that they'll reflect in due time.

You may be making this step too linear.

Yes, in the algorithm I just shared—in a utopian world—someone would return and reflect with you on a specific issue you coached them on, and then the issue would be tied with a neat and tidy bow.

But the Return and Reflect step can be used at any time, even if there was no specific coaching before it. For example, I make proactive calls to my clients about a week before their session, so we're on the same page with the hot issues and how the quarter went. Invariably during this call, I ask, "How's the team? Are they ready for next week?" These questions cause the leader to pause and think, *How is my team? Are they ready for next week?* Then they discuss the quarter, reflecting on the stories and events they experienced. This call certainly gives me the information I need, but the real benefit is that by creating the space for this leader to reflect on the quarter, they become clearer about their issues and what to focus on for next quarter. I didn't need to do any coaching before and the reflection was useful.

Make it a habit.

Make reflections part of your normal meetings. If you have regularly scheduled one-on-one meetings, ask "What would be helpful to reflect on during our time together?" If you run on EOS, you'll hold Quarterly Conversations™ where you'll create a space for your team to reflect on what's working and what's not.

Set a date.

When I have a critical coaching session that must have a follow-up, I ask the leader to commit to a day and time for returning and reflecting. We put it on the calendar to make space for it before we leave the conversation.

2. Reflect

When they do return, ask your people to *reflect* vs. *report*. A report is just a statement of facts or a replay of what happened. Get them focused on reflecting on what happened. Help them think deeper about observations, behaviors, aha moments, etc., that will serve them in multiple situations, not only this one. When they do the talking, the lessons stick.

This can be as simple as asking, "How did it go?" If they are ready to go deeper, you can ask, "What did you learn? On reflection, when did you know this project was off track? What will you do differently next time?" Bosses want to know the outcome of the issue. Coaches want to help people learn lessons for the future. Do both! Spend most of the time in reflection rather than reporting, and they'll start to think faster.

Here are some ways that you can create great spaces for using the power of reflection to enable the experience to stick.

Hold Regular Reflection Sessions

A reflection session is a chunk of defined time dedicated to reflection and celebration. It's a space that invites open and honest feedback, involves curiosity and truth-telling, and encourages verbal acknowledgement and celebration of wins. And it doesn't take much time at all for these to be very effective. They can focus on a timespan (*Reflect on the last 90 days*) or they can be about something specific (*What did we learn from our last version launch?*).

Step One—The Question

At a very general and simple level, you can ask, "How did it go?" This is open-ended and allows the other person to take the answer wherever they want. An upgrade to this question is "What did you learn?" This gets them to think at a deeper, more intrinsic level.

To really add clarity, ask the question as a distinction, using opposite ends of a spectrum on their reflections: "What worked, and what didn't work? What did you like; what didn't you like? What was easy, and what was hard?" I've noticed that when I ask the question based on the distinction, this produces the deepest level of thinking. This question gives a tighter framework or direction to the brain, so the brain can find the answers more quickly.

This step is brief, and often takes less than 30 seconds. All you need to do is ask the question, give simple instructions for step two, and let the brain do the rest!

Step Two—Five Quiet Minutes

After asking the question, give your people five quiet minutes to think about the answers to the question, and then ask them to write the answers down. Directions for this section include

- There are no wrong answers.
- There is no requirement of content.
- You can write one thing or fifteen things.
- You must write it down.

There are three main cognitive functions going on during this step.

Recall

The thinking brain actively engages in remembering past events, feelings, activities, and conversations. The more opportunity we give our brains to recall events, the faster it'll work and the more accurate the memories will be.

Elevation

As the brain looks back on an event or a time period, it naturally sees highlights and meaningful moments. As it recalls these, it metaphorically rises above the situation and can observe it from an outsider's perspective. People who reflect can observe their actions or reactions outside the heat of the moment.

Logic

Something powerful happens when you're asked to put your thoughts into words. By moving the memory through the brain's logical prefrontal cortex where our language center is, the thought becomes more rational, more true, more realistic, and more clear. Just the act of deciding what to write down increases the validity and effectiveness of the reflection.

During the five-quiet-minutes portion of a recent reflection session with a new client, I noticed that one of the leaders wasn't writing down his thoughts. When I encouraged him to write as he was thinking, he said he had bad penmanship, so he didn't like to write. When we started sharing what each of us had written, his thoughts were unclear, he rambling, and he was disappointed that he didn't see the positivity in the situation as the rest of the team did. The next time we had a reflection session, I encouraged him to write, even if he couldn't read his handwriting. The second time around, he shared with the group that he was stunned at his clarity and how much more confidence he had in the company's growth in the last quarter.

Step Three—Share What You Wrote with Someone Else

This can be simple—participants read from the page they wrote on—or complex—participants discuss, in depth, each thing they wrote. When time is limited, I ask people just to share one thing they wrote. When you ask someone to choose one or two items to share, their brain now needs to filter everything they reflected on and decide which is the most significant reflection. When this occurs, what they share is tagged in the brain as significant enough to store to memory. This is how we take advantage of the experiences that people have within our company. This is how we create a company that has the Thinking Advantage.

Types of Reflection Sessions

1. One-on-one

These sessions are intense and effective and can get to the heart of the impact of the event quickly. This is what you experience when you have a personal coach or a trusted friendship. Reflecting with one person also opens the door for the coach or boss to do additional teaching in a private setting. If the reflections aren't clear, you can help bring clarity. If the reflections show that some thinking is very reactive, you can jump into helping them choose a different response. When the reflecting is mostly negative, you can help reframe the event with them as a learning for the future. This type of reflection is built into EOS as the Quarterly Conversation. Some teams find this type of reflection so valuable that they like to do one-on-one sessions weekly! This is a perfect time for reflecting, not only reporting.

2. In Groups

Group reflections take on a broader type of learning because we reflect with each other, hearing what was important or experienced from a wider perspective. This is where we can learn from each other and multiply ourselves without having to experience the event ourselves. I also find that when several members observe the same findings in group reflections, it helps build a sense of unity. When they're on opposite sides of the topic, the reflection offers a powerful moment for understanding each other.

When we reflect as a group, we have more teachers in the room. Doing the math indicates more experiences and more knowledge to pull from than when reflecting with only one person. We can help each other reflect on our understanding of the event and get multiple perspectives and other opinions. Often, when I hold group reflection sessions, leaders on these teams walk away more confident because they've confirmed that either everyone was seeing the quarter the same way or, if they saw the quarter differently, they were able to clear up misunderstandings and get back in the same boat.

One of my personal favorite group reflection sessions happens when I go to my Strategic Coach quarterly sessions. I get to reflect with the best group of entrepreneurs on the planet (in my humble opinion). Going into the session, I'm never sure what I'll create, and that's part of the excitement. Every time I go, I come away with new insights about myself, my clients, entrepreneurs, and humans in general. Most of this is realized while I'm reflecting with my peers, both when I'm listening to them reflect and when they are listening to me reflect as we apply the day's teachings.

Pro Tip

Not all peer groups can be counted on for successful reflection. I tried several different options before finally finding a match at Strategic Coach. Now that I know the substantial benefit I get from this group, it's worth the effort I put in to making sure it was the right one for me. If you've outgrown your peer group, I encourage you to invest in finding a higher quality group. It may be time for an upgrade!

3. Self-reflection Sessions

This is simply where you do some reflecting on your own about a specific event, situation, or issue from which you'd like to extract some clarity or insight. This can take the form of simple journaling or a formal Clarity Break.

Warning: For this to be effective, you must *write* as you self-reflect. Otherwise, this has a chance to turn into rumination. Remember, rumination leads to unproductive worrying and worrying is a horrible use of the creative human mind, so if you choose to use self-reflection, do it on purpose. Schedule a time, make a date with yourself, be purposeful with what you want out of your reflection session, and be disciplined with capturing your thoughts—positive and negative—on paper.

Because talking through our reflections is so effective in creating aha moments of learning, finding someone to talk to even after your reflection session will yield the greatest results.

WORRYING IS A HORRIBLE USE OF THE CREATIVE HUMAN MIND

Pro Tip

When leading or participating in reflection sessions, keep in mind the power of celebration. Regularly look for wins to celebrate, even if the learning or aha moment is small. This utilizes the "celebration technique" described by BJ Fogg in his best-selling book *Tiny Habits*. This Stanford behavior scientist teaches that the more often we celebrate our wins, the more we get addicted to winning. If we can get our brains addicted to positive behaviors, this increases our capacity for creative, productive thinking.

When people feel good after a reflection session with you, they'll want to do it again, making it easier to get them to engage in reflection. Plus, the serotonin, adrenaline, and oxytocin that make us feel awesome while winning are the antidotes to cortisol, the stress hormone that inhibits critical thinking.

Teach Someone Else

When I was 15 years old, I started my first official teaching job—teaching two-year-olds. When I was recently reflecting on this job with a friend, I jovially mentioned that I think I did more entertaining than teaching! She then remarked, "Isn't entertainment a big part of teaching?" Yes. I guess it is. I approached this new job with what came natural to me: singing, dancing, being silly, running, jumping, and overall enthusiasm. I also approached it with what I already knew from my training classes from the Child Care Association and in high school.

A few years later, when I was teaching five-year-olds, I did a science experiment in my high school science class about the water cycle. I thought, *My five-year-olds would love this! Could I really teach them high school science?* I obsessed over this for the next few days and found a way to simplify the experiment and put it into steps they'd understand.

As I prepared to teach the kids, I started to ask myself more in-depth questions. I tried the simplified experiment until I had it in a format that would work for them, and I started to observe in a different way than I had as a student in my science class. I was so engaged with the subject that my teacher noticed and asked me to tell the class what I was doing. It wasn't until years later that I realized that by engaging in *teaching*, I learned so much more than I did while being taught. I still use this skill today in my coaching practice.

Here's how I now learn as I teach. I call it my creation cycle:

1. Consume

I am an active student. I consume books, audiobooks, and podcasts. I attend classes, take courses, hire coaches, have rich conversations with strangers, and belong to high-quality peer groups. This is all raw data for what I'm about to create.

2. Try It

During my coaching sessions (in the Co-create Mode), I offer (or teach) what I've learned during my consumption of the raw data. This comes in the form of retelling a story, phrase, or principle I learned, or simply guiding someone to a resource or book that might be helpful. It's more than a bit of a miracle that I seem to learn something just as the client needs me to share it with them!

3. Ask If It Was Effective

If the information or comment was effective, I take note—I may use it again. If it wasn't, I also take note. I'll usually try something three to five times before I throw it out or put it back into the raw data category to be morphed into something else in the future.

4. Ponder It

When something is repeatedly effective, I start writing about it, thinking about it, and talking about it with peers. I often ask myself a *why* question or formulate some kind of hypothesis with a few bullet points. And I keep teaching it as it iterates.

5. Publish it

This is the scary part, but it's necessary to see if the concept resonates with a wider population than my clients. This can come in the form of a quick video recorded and posted on LinkedIn or a blog, or a specific session I've been asked to present for peers or clients.

6. Simplify It

After getting feedback from people who interact with the concept, if it's still feeling really useful, I'll simplify the creation: I find a pattern, add sticky titles, or name the concept. This often comes with a visual model as well.

7. Iterate

It's never really done. Sometimes, the creation changes or morphs as I teach it each time. I'll try a new analogy or share a new story that works even better than the previous story. Occasionally, it becomes part of other things I teach or create. As I'm teaching, my understanding is always changing, so the things I create can also evolve and change. They don't need to be done, and that keeps me away from hoping they will ever be perfect.

8. Commit

Sometimes, when concepts are compelling, I commit to get them to an even wider audience, like publishing them in a book (ahem ... this book ☺). As I write, I'm thinking about how the reader will ingest the information. What should come first? What stories are the best to share that will help the reader learn the concept? To help my creation cycle continue, I add deadlines and milestones that other people are involved in that add pressure to my thinking. I create and iterate disciplines that require me to think about the topic on the deepest level yet.

As my coach, Dan Sullivan, says, "If you want the energy to create the show, sell the ticket first!" (By the way, I read that quote this morning before I wrote this section of the book. I read it just in time for this section—miraculous!) When I commit to writing a book or teaching a new course, it pulls the creation cycle forward. I have a deadline, and I know someone is waiting on me to produce.

If you're a geek like me, you may be thinking, *This is just the scientific method!* Yep, it is. And guess what—I didn't even realize that until someone pointed it out to me. It took someone from outside of my creation cycle to observe what was really happening, but it sure gave me confidence in my process knowing that other creators and scientists are using a similar process.

Consider these additional ideas that show that teaching something requires deeper thinking:

- *You must reflect on what you know in order to teach it.*
  Teaching something automatically asks the brain

to reflect on what it already knows and to organize those points in a way that can be communicated effectively.

- *Apply a little pressure.* The right amount of pressure brings out the best in people. With a little pressure on someone to perform, their attention is more tightly focused, and adrenaline helps the neural pathways form in a more permanent way.

- *You must prepare.* In most cases, the teacher will need to prepare to teach others. Effective preparation involves thinking and practicing. When we engage in deliberate practice, our brains tag the information as useful for the future.

- *You must think about how others are going to receive it.* This now becomes about others instead of all about you. When teaching others, you'll think about how to do it in the most simple, effective way to communicate the topic and engage the participants.

- *You must sell yourself.* This means that when you teach something effectively, you need to believe it yourself. Occasionally, when called on to teach a topic you aren't sold on, you'll need to understand it more profoundly to buy in before teaching it. If there are contradictions or you aren't invested, it creates the space for deep thought and deep conversations with others who are. When you've come full circle, from non-belief to belief, this creates a powerful story for sharing as you teach.

- *Get back to the basics.* There is more pressure to have a deeper understanding of a topic's foundational principles if you're going to teach them. Teaching basics takes you back to foundational principles and checks your understanding. You'll get a chance to answer your questions as you prepare to answer your learners' questions.

- *Your confidence will increase.* As you repeatedly teach a topic and apply it, your confidence increases. As your confidence increases, you'll be able to take more risks with additional thinking and topics.

- *The boss is not king.* Perhaps my most favorite reason for asking others to engage in reflection via teaching others is that the boss isn't seen as the sole source of information. When the information is shared and taught by other people in the organization, the burden of being the only one in the department/company with all the information or all the solution-and-creation power decreases. Rather, the thinking is shared by many teachers in the company on a variety of topics.

- *Use a variety of styles and approaches.* By asking people to extend their thinking and reflecting by teaching, it creates a benefit for the rest of the company: they can learn from different people who have different styles and different approaches. Adult brains respond to novelty and variety with a little adrenaline and a heightened sense of attention. When there is a variety of sources, the learner learns more!

REFLECTION SECTION

(Isn't it fun that we're about to reflect on the power of reflection?)

1. Flip back through the previous Reflection Sections. From what you wrote in these sections, what became clearer to you?

    _____

    _____

2. What thoughts do you have now that you didn't have before you spent time reflecting?

    _____

    _____

3. Think about the spaces you create for reflection currently (both for yourself and your people). Which of these are more effective than others?

    _____

    _____

4. Where could you upgrade from reporting to reflection?

    _____

    _____

5. How effective is your current peer group? Does it create a space for reflection? If not, is it time for an upgrade?

    _____

    _____

6. Name a few people you've noticed who are really effective at creating space for reflection. What do they do that you'd like to emulate?

_____

_____

CONCLUSION

In the summer of 2020, I become more convinced than ever of the practice of deep reflection via teaching as I took on a role with EOS Worldwide as the Western Region Community Builder. This is a long title that includes, as one of my duties, training new EOS Implementers. I'm responsible for training them on delivering the EOS message in the purest way as they connect with prospects, host their first sessions, and build their businesses.

It had been over six years since I went through that training myself, and I'd evolved to using my personal style in working with my clients as I iterated with what worked and what worked even better. Coming back to the foundational basics blew my ever-loving mind! As I prepared to teach, I quickly became aware that the fundamentals I was using had become automatic. There were also skills I had once mastered but become lazy with.

As I poured myself into the materials with a fresh perspective, I became re-sold on the power of the basics. As I listened to and coached the new Implementers through their worries, stories, and aspirations, I became more invested in the power of the beginner's mindset. I had come full circle (several times) through the ups and downs of being a coach, and they were here, just beginning! They were ready to start their journey with their own ups and downs. I learned to honor that beginner's mindset by not over-teaching and by sharing additional teachings when they were ready for them (and not a minute sooner). All of this took an extreme amount of reflecting. I've never been more exhausted and fulfilled at the same time. Pouring your energy into teaching others is a calorie-burning activity!

Although it's the last step in this algorithm, Return and Reflect is actually an ongoing step that can be used at any time. It brings clarity, confidence, and direction when done alone or with others. If you've been thinking deeply while you've been reading this book, and if I've triggered a section of your brain that loves to engage with deep thinking, you may enjoy this upgrade to the algorithm you just learned. Be warned. It might blow your mind! ☺

What if it's not a four-step algorithm but a continuous loop?

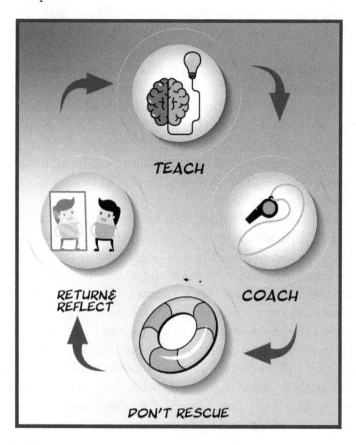

⇨ I teach.

⇨ I coach.

⇨ I don't rescue.

⇨ I invite others to return and reflect …

⇨ … which leads to additional teaching opportunities. Sometimes I ask the one who learned to teach the whole organization what they just learned …

⇨ … so we can coach each other on what was taught, finding solutions together.

⇨ Then, we stop rescuing each other and, instead, support one another.

⇨ This invites regular reflection as a way to ask "What else needs to be taught?"

⇨ So, we enroll new SMEs (subject matter experts) to do the teaching and update the Company University documents based on what they just learned as they reflected on their experiences with trying something out of their comfort zone …

⇨ … and reflecting on what they learned about those adrenaline-spiking experiences.

⇨ And so on, and so forth …

Would living in a company like this help you solve more issues at their root? Would it create a company that regularly takes advantage of opportunities before its competitors do? Would it help you focus on results and provide space for the leadership team to see and plan even further into the future, leading to bigger and better results? Would it create a learning and thinking company that continually multiplies itself?

My experience is that it will, and it does. Will you join me in creating thinkers in our entrepreneurial companies? Will you join me in teaching our people how to think? Will you join me in ushering in a new era of work, where the thinkers will be the engine that fuels the wins, the solutions, and the productivity that our world is longing for? Will your company lead your industry with the Thinking Advantage? The only thing we need to ask ourselves is "What will we teach them first?"

Here's to your optimized, beautiful, and powerful brain that will pull us all into a bigger, brighter future!

ACKNOWLEDGMENTS

First things first: I'm nothing without having been "born on third base." I am so grateful for my entrepreneurial roots that go back many generations. This book was made possible because I got to stand on the shoulders of quiet, hard-working giants of humans that I call family.

If you've ever been to my session room, you'll know that I often say, "This is where the magic happens!" I could not write with such confidence had I not experienced the impact of the lessons and insights in this book in the session room with willing clients who love to experiment. I am humbled every day by the chance to work with all of you! Thank you for being willing to create magic with me! Yes, the results are rewarding, but watching you win with the solutions we co-create is awe-inspiring.

How many right people in the right seats does it take to produce a book like this? Five on my team and one amazing publisher with a proven process! Lindsey, Stephanie, Leslie, Colin, and Morgan made sure that all the pieces kept moving, and Kary Oberbrunner and his team at Author Academy Elite made sure this book got to you! I hope our partnership lasts until 2100!

And, finally, to my colleagues and coaches—your encouragement, challenges, and thought-provoking questions keep me on the road to fulfilling my purpose: to spread joy by being useful and generous.

And I can't forget Thor, the God of Thunder! I'm sure everyone would miss him if he weren't acknowledged!

APPENDICES

The Thinking Advantage
COURSE

This is a day-long workshop for company leaders in growth mode.

During this workshop, we explore the mindsets it takes to be a boss who creates an accountable culture. After participating in the workshop, managers feel confident in their ability to activate the productivity

» on their team
» in their department
» or for the entire company

Designed strictly for management, this session can be held with multiple companies in attendance or customized for an individual organization.

INTERACTIVE WORKSHOP: 5-7 HOURS
LIVE KEYNOTE: 60-90 MINUTES

Visit JillYoung.com to sign up your leaders today!

LIVE KEYNOTES & WORKSHOPS

The Earning Advantage: Introduce everyone in your company to the Earning Advantage mindset.

In this interactive workshop, you'll discover

» how productivity affects the engagement levels of the company

» how to identify productivity killers

» how to offer resources that will help employees understand how they contribute to the company.

The workshop encourages participants to develop a deeper commitment to serving others so all team members can work toward the organization's success.

INTERACTIVE WORKSHOP: 2-4 HOURS
LIVE KEYNOTE: 60-90 MINUTES

The Courage Advantage: Staring Down the Fear of Moving to Mastery

In this four-hour workshop, leaders discover

» how to identify where fear is active in their leadership role and their company culture

» a four-step map of the stages of courage and how each stage lulls us to stay there

» the action steps needed to move us closer to mastery of our fears

INTERACTIVE WORKSHOP: 4 HOURS
LIVE KEYNOTE: 60-90 MINUTES

Get a Grip: Are You Running Your Company or Is Your Company Running You?

This workshop provides an introduction to how to run your company on the Entrepreneurial Operating System (EOS).

INTERACTIVE WORKSHOP: 3 HOURS
LIVE KEYNOTE: 90 MINUTES

Sign up today at JillYoung.com!

EOS
IMPLEMENTATION

Will the Entrepreneurial Operating System (EOS) work for you? Consider these questions:

- » Is the company hitting the ceiling?
- » Is the company changing direction often?
- » Do you get one answer from one manager and a different response from another manager?
- » Could the company benefit from more accountability and discipline?
- » Could the company be more cohesive, open, and honest?
- » Does the owner or leadership team want to improve?

If any of these questions resonate with you, contact me at Jill@JillYoung.com

OTHER BOOKS
BY JILL YOUNG

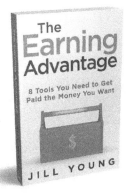

The Earning Advantage:
8 Tools You Need to Get Paid
the Money You Want

The Courage Advantage:

3 Mindsets Your Team Needs
to Cultivate Fierce Discipline,
Incredible Fun, and a Culture
of Experimentation

JILL YOUNG

CPSIA information can be obtained
at www.ICGtesting.com
Printed in the USA
BVHW032247071021
618416BV00002B/5